Crazy Gary's Mobile Disco

Gary Owen

Methuen Drama

Methuen Drama

First published in Great Britain in 2001by Methuen Drama
Methuen Publishing Ltd

ISBN 0 413 76850 3

A CIP catalogue record for this book is available at the British Library

Typeset by SX Composing DTP, Rayleigh, Essex
Transferred to digital printing 2004

Paines Plough and Sgript Cymru

present the premiere of

CRAZY GARY'S MOBILE DISCO

by Gary Owen

First performed at Chapter Arts Centre, 8 February 2001

INTRODUCTION

Crazy Gary's Mobile Disco is Gary Owen's first play. It was not a commission; it was, instead, one of those rare jewels that drop onto your desk one morning. (Actually, it dropped onto John Tiffany's desk at the Traverse Theatre in Edinburgh, who reluctantly, due to its Welshness and not Scottishness, sent it on to me. Thank you, John.)

Gary definitely has the secret ingredient – a voice, the ability to take us to a complicated, passionate, political place with humanity, emotion and humour. This, coupled with a great talent for storytelling and craft, makes *Crazy Gary's Mobile Disco* very compelling. Rarely have a town, its inhabitants and the dark lives beneath the surface been so dramatically and effectively evoked.

It returns to that most theatrical of forms, the monologue; an actor standing in front of you – the audience – and including you, willing you to be part of their story, and responding to your mood, your understanding.

We are delighted to be producing this in collaboration with Sgript Cymru. I hope you enjoy it.

Vicky Featherstone
Paines Plough

Note: The playscript that follows was correct at the time of going to press, but may have changed during rehearsal.

CRAZY GARY'S MOBILE DISCO

by Gary Owen

CAST

Gary	David Rees Talbot
Mathew D. Melody	Steven Meo
Russell Markham	Richard Mylan

Director	Vicky Featherstone
Designer	Georgia Sion
Lighting Designer	Natasha Chivers

Production Manager	Jo Manser
Company Stage Manager	Chloë Wibaut

Publicity Photograph	Rose Jones
Production Photography	Manuel Harlan
Press Representatives	**for Paines Plough:**
	Chamberlain McAuley
	020 8858 5545
	for Sgript Cymru:
	PS Media
	02920 451 168

Leaflet/Poster and Cover Design

Eureka! Design Consultants Ltd

With thanks to the Bridewell Theatre; Tom Meeten; Mike Donnelly; Dave Brown; Sam Barrett and Steve, for making our offices a great place to work.

THE COMPANY

Gary Owen – Writer

Gary Owen was educated at Brynteg Comprehensive School in Bridgend, Sidney Sussex College, Cambridge, and at the European Film College in Denmark. Formerly a script editor for BBC Wales Drama, Gary was part of the team which created *Station Road* and *Belonging*. *Crazy Gary's Mobile Disco* is Gary's first piece for the stage. His second play, *The Shadow of a Boy*, was written while on attachment to the National Theatre Studio. Gary's network debut, *Alister Meek Gets a Result* went out in autumn 2000 as part of Channel 4's 'Dogma TV' season, and he's now working on a screen-adaptation of *Crazy Gary's Mobile Disco*, commissioned by BBC Wales. Throughout 2001, Gary will be Paines Plough's Writer-in-Residence, a post supported by the Pearson Playwrights' Scheme and sponsored by the Peggy Ramsay Foundation. Gary was a founding member of the Then Jerico fan club.

Natasha Chivers – Lighting Designer

Natasha trained at the London Academy of Music and Dramatic Art.

Work includes: *Firebird* (Unicorn at the Pleasance); *The Body of a Woman* (Young Vic Studio); *Among Broken Hearts* (Traverse, Edinburgh and Highland Tour); *The Prisoner of Zenda* and *Death and the Maiden* (Watermill, Newbury); *The Blue Zone* (Birmingham Royal Ballet and Frantic Assembly); *The Salt Garden* (Strathcona); *Into our Dreams* (Almeida Education Project); *Tristan and Isolde* (Camberwell Pocket Opera); *A Wake for Miss Montreal* (Chelsea Centre); *The Reel of the Hanged Man* (Traverse, Tron and Tour); *Hymns and Service Charge* (Frantic Assembly); *Sweet Dreams* (Sphinx) and *Demons and Dybbuks* (Method and Madness, Young Vic).

In 2001, Natasha will also be working on *Notre-Dame de Paris* (Strathcona Theatre Company) and *Listening Heaven* (Royal Lyceum, Edinburgh).

Vicky Featherstone – Director

Vicky Featherstone is Artistic Director of Paines Plough. For Paines Plough: *Splendour* by Abi Morgan (Fringe First and Herald Angel), *Riddance* by Linda McLean (Fringe First and Herald Angel), *The Cosmonaut's Last Message to the Woman He Once Loved in the Former Soviet Union* by David Greig, *Crave* by Sarah Kane, *Sleeping Around* by Stephen Greenhorn, Hilary Fannin, Abi Morgan and Mark Ravenhill, and *Crazyhorse* by Parv Bancil.

She has directed *Outside Now* by David Greig, *The Moment is a Gift That's Why It's Called the Present* by Abi Morgan, *Too Cold for Snow* by Michael Wynne, and most recently *Fortune* by Abi Morgan, David Greig, Michael Wynne and Danny Brown, for Prada as part of Milan Fashion Week.

She has also directed *Anna Weiss* for the Traverse Theatre (Fringe First and Scotland on Sunday's Critic's Award). Other work includes script development for United Film and Television Productions, where she created *Where the Heart Is* and developed *Touching Evil*; previously Script Development Executive for Granada Television Drama and, currently, Script Development Consultant for the BBC.

Jo Manser – Production Manager
Jo is Production Manager for Primitive Science and has worked on *Icarus Falling*, *Poseidon* and *Hunger* for production at international festivals. Other work includes Designer on *Para Active* for the Passo a Passo Dance Co. and *Eating Raoul* for the New and Abused Theatre Co. at the Bridewell Theatre. He also lectures regularly at the Wimbledon School of Art and the Central School of Speech and Drama.

Steven Meo – Mathew D. Melody
Theatre includes *Flesh and Blood* (Sherman and Hampstead Theatre); *Up 'n' Under* (Bristol Old Vic); *Metamorphosis* (Merlin Theatre, Budapest); *East from the Gantry* (Edinburgh Festival) and *Woyzeck* (Wyeside Theatre).

For the Welsh College of Music and Drama: *Into the Woods*, *Three Sisters*, *The Clearing* and *The Man of Mode* (all for Bute Theatre).

For television: *Belonging*, Series 1 and 2 (BBC Wales); *Score* (BBC1); *Without Motive* (HTV Network); *Nice Girl* (BBC2); *Comedy Pilot* and *The Slate* (BBC Wales).

For radio: *Fallen*; *The Owl Service* (BBC Radio 4); *A Bedroom Farce* (WCMD) and *Seven Good Stories* (Tretower Court).

Richard Mylan – Russell Markham
Theatre includes *Badfinger* (Donmar Warehouse), *Starlight Express* (Trevor Nunn) and *The Shoot* (James Lance).

Television includes *Belonging* (BBC), *Welcome to Orty Fou* (Carlton), *The Bill* (Thames), *Border Café* (Hartswood), *Dirty Work* (Douglas McKinnon), *Couples* (LWT), *Casualty* (BBC1), *Tech Heads* (Celador), *Silent Witness* (BBC1), *The Demon Headmaster* (BBC) and *Beer Goggles* (David McKenzie).

Films include *Score* (Andy De Emmony); *Love, Peace and Pancake* (Roma Kuhn); *Check-out Girl* (Rupert Graves); *Snarl Up* (Michael Winterbottom); *Dead on Time* (James Larkin); *The Wisdom of Crocodiles* (Puci Leong) and *Speak Like a Child* (John Akomfrah).

Georgia Sion – Designer
Georgia trained on the Motley Theatre Design Course.

Theatre includes *Crave*; *Sleeping Around* and *The Cosmonaut's Last Message to the Woman He Once Loved in the Former Soviet Union* for Paines Plough; *Arabian Nights* (Young Vic and Broadway); *Caravan* (National Theatre of Norway); *Perfect Days* and *Abandonment* (Traverse Theatre); *Afore Night Come* (Theatre Clwyd); *Goldmines* (Clean Break Theatre Company); *The Weavers* (The Gate Theatre); *Twelfth Night* (Central School of Speech and Drama); *Othello* (Watermill Theatre); *The Sunset Ship* (Young Vic Theatre Co.); *Shift* (Old Red Lion); *Cut and Running* (BAC); *Lovers* (RSC Fringe Festival); *Two Clouds Over Eden* (Royal Exchange) and *The Importance of Being Earnest* (Nottingham Playhouse).

Opera includes *A Ronne*, *A Medicine for Melancholy* and *Saints and Cities* (ENO, Baylis Programme); *King and Marshall* (Bloomsbury Theatre) and *Four Saints in Three Acts* (Trinity Opera).

David Rees Talbot – Gary
Theatre includes *Sleeping Beauty* (Unicorn Arts Theatre); *A View to a Skill* (Chrysalis Theatre Co.); *Little Country, Big War* (Museum of Welsh Life, St Fagans); *The Crucible* (Theatre Einon) and *Les Liaisons Dangereuses*; *Company*; *The Clearing* and *The Assassins* for the Welsh College of Music and Drama.

Television includes *Score* (BBC); *High Hopes* (BBC Wales) and *Learning the Language* (HTV Wales).

Chloë Wibaut – Company Stage Manager
After graduating from Guildford School of Acting in June 1999, Chloë stage-managed a season of weekly rep. at Frinton Summer Theatre. She then became Assistant Stage Manager at the Swan Theatre in Worcester, and at the Almeida, working on *The Room* and *Celebration*, directed by Harold Pinter. Most recently, Chloë worked at the Millennium Dome, stage-managing the central show.

PAINES PLOUGH

Paines Plough has been discovering outstanding new voices in British theatre for twenty-five years. Funded by the Arts Council of England, we produce two new plays a year and tour them throughout the UK. As the driving force behind the company has always been the vision of the playwright, we have created a programme of work to access, support and develop the most exciting voices nationally.

Since Vicky Featherstone's appointment as Artistic Director in 1997, we have produced *Splendour* by Abi Morgan, which won a Fringe First and a Herald Angel Award at the Edinburgh Festival 2000, *Riddance* by Linda McLean (Fringe First and a Herald Angel), *The Cosmonaut's Last Message to the Woman He Once Loved in the Former Soviet Union* by David Greig, *Crave* by Sarah Kane, *Sleeping Around* by Hilary Fannin, Stephen Greenhorn, Abi Morgan and Mark Ravenhill, *Crazyhorse* by Parv Bancil and *The Wolves* by Michael Punter.

'Ticket to Write', funded by the National Lottery, is our nation-wide playwriting programme. A partnership between Paines Plough and four major regional theatres, it finds, commissions and produces the best new writing talent in those regions. Through this programme, Paines Plough has discovered, commissioned and developed forty new writers and produced and toured forty short plays. Ticket to Write recently completed its final phase with the West Yorkshire Playhouse in the autumn of 2000, when we produced ten short plays by black and Asian writers from Yorkshire.

'Wild Lunch' is now a regular festival of script-in-hand performances. Born out of a selected writers' group, the latest festival, 'Jubilee – Plays from Underground', was presented in collaboration with the BBC New Writing Initiative in early summer 2000. One of these plays, *Stratford* by Debbie Green, was produced by Paines Plough and presented at the Soho Theatre in October 2000 as part of their autumn lunchtime season.

Coming Soon

In summer and autumn 2001, Paines Plough will collaborate with the much-acclaimed Frantic Assembly on a new play by Abi Morgan.

SGRIPT CYMRU
Contemporary Drama Wales

Formed in May 2000, Sgript Cymru is the national new-writing company for Wales, working in both Welsh and English.

'A Welsh theatre is necessary to reveal us to ourselves.' Harri Webb

For the first time, Wales has a company whose mission is to discover, develop and produce the best work of contemporary Welsh or Wales-based playwrights.

Sgript Cymru emerged out of the successful Welsh-language company Dalier Sylw, under the leadership of Artistic Director Bethan Jones, which enjoyed ten years of championing a fresh generation of Welsh-language playwrights, such as Gareth Miles, Sion Eirian, Geraint Lewis and Meic Povey, to audiences throughout Wales. Now Sgript Cymru has incorporated Associate Director, Simon Harris, who brings his extensive experience to the company, after successes as a freelance writer and director with *Badfinger* and *Nothing to Pay* for his company, Thin Language.

As part of its core activity, Sgript Cymru commissions new plays in Welsh and in English, regularly hosts a development forum for new work called Sgript Xplosure! showcasing the work of dozens of new writers, presents its own productions, such as *Yr Hen Blant* by Meic Povey and *Art and Guff* by Cath Tregenna, and also works in co-production with companies such as Paines Plough.

In addition, the company supports writer development from grass-root level – through schemes such as our vibrant Young Writers' Group, and community access through our Writer-in-Residence initiative – to individual contact with our Literary Department.

'Sgript Cymru . . . [provides] an invaluable resource to writers in Wales.' www.theatre-wales.co.uk

Sgript Cymru is absolutely committed to producing high-quality new plays that bring to light the best theatre writing that Wales can offer and revealing it to audiences in Wales and beyond.

PAINES PLOUGH

Vicky Featherstone
Artistic Director

Belinda Hamilton
Administrative Director

Caroline Newall
Administrator

Lucy Morrison
Literary Associate

Paines Plough
4th Floor
43 Aldwych
London WC2B 4DN

Tel: +44 (0) 20 7240 4533
Fax: +44 (0) 20 7240 4534
office@painesplough.com

SGRIPT CYMRU

Bethan Jones
Artistic Director

Mai Jones
Administrative Director

Simon Harris
Associate Director

Bill Hopkinson
Literary Manager

Sgript Cymru
Chapter
Market Road
Canton
Cardiff CF5 1QE

Tel: +44 (0) 29 2023 6650
Fax: +44 (0) 29 2023 6651
sgriptcymru@sgriptcymru.com

CRAZY GARY'S MOBILE DISCO

Tour Dates 2001

8-17 February
Chapter Arts Centre
Cardiff

20 February
Queen's Hall Arts Centre
Hexham

22-24 February
Clwyd Theatr Cymru
Mold

27-28 February
Live Theatre
Newcastle

2 March
Taliesin Arts Centre
Swansea

3 March
Aberystwyth Arts Centre

6-7 March
Theatre in the Mill
Bradford

8-10 March
Contact
Manchester

12 March-7 April
Lyric Studio
Hammersmith

17-18 April
Old Town Hall
Hemel Hempstead

19-21 April
Studio Leicester Haymarket

24-25 April
Stamford Arts Centre

27-28 April
Gardner Arts Centre
University of Sussex
Brighton

30 April-1 May
South Hill Park
Bracknell

2 May
The Point Dance
& Arts Centre
Eastleigh

4-5 May
Stephen Joseph Theatre
Scarborough

diolch: Carole Byrne Jones, Andrea Smith, John Hefin, Gala Antipenko, Joachim Trier, Christina Rosendahl, Rob Storr, James Topping, Craig Russell, Angharad Herbert, Gilly Adams, Winsome Pinnock, Pedr James, Maggie Russell, Michael McCoy, Jessica Dromgoole, Vicky Featherstone and all my family.

for: all the weapons-grade honeys who've been inappropriately handled, 1989–2001: you can take this as one great big hey look I'm really really sorry.

1: booty call

Here comes **Gary** *and he is an a-hole, oh yes he is. He has a big fob of keys which should be for a supercharged Capri or Manta with die-faster stripes but are actually for his white Escort van. Every now and again he throws the keys a foot in the air then swipes them back into his hand, and whenever he does this there's a greasy smile like he's just accomplished some impressive feat of manual dexterity. I think he is probably not the most giving or sensitive of lovers.*

He swaggers and pulls out a phone, the kind you have to unfold. He opens it up. Goes to dial –

– and loses his nerve. He works up a new facial expression, all smiley and approachable, and tries again. He punches two digits –

– and chickens out again, snapping the phone closed. Puts some effort into what he thinks might be glacial cool, and gets as far as dialling the whole number. But as the call is about to connect, his cool crumbles and he stabs at the little red button. He's pretty pissed off.

Right. Fuck it. I'm gonna fucking spoil it for you all. I'm gonna tell you how this story ends right now.

When I was growing up there was all this – nuclear paranoia shit. All this – 'If the air-raid warning came what would you do, if you only had three minutes to live?'

If I only had three minutes left to live, I'd carry on just as I am. Because in three minutes' time, I'm gonna be fucking . . . in heaven.

I'm gonna be fucking the fittest chick in the whole wide bastard world.

So sod all that 'will he get her, won't he get her' bullshit – I'm telling you now, this all ends with me pulling the perfect girl.

Goes to dial, then thinks better of it.

I didn't have anything to do till a crucial business appointment at ten, so I flicked on *Crimewatch* and occupied myself giving detailed descriptions of people I hate to detectives working this harrowing multiple murder case.

Half-nine I have to give it up. I've provided Her Majesty's thickest with a hundred and forty-two invaluable new leads and they're getting a bit suspicious – my voice is . . . kind of familiar from somewhere. It's a real bastard – there's so many people you hate but, like old Nick says, only really a couple of multiple murderers on the go at any one time.

So I fuck off out the house and head down the Boar's Head, where a very different kind of crime is taking place. It's not a straightforward breaking of the law of the land. It's not a crime against humanity. It's much worse than that.

It's a crime . . . against disco.

Thursday night, down the Boar's Head, is disco night. Every fucker knows that. Every fucker, it seems, except Brian the bitch of a landlord, who has decided to replace the disco with . . . kara-fuckin-oke. Kara-fuckin-oke run by a ginger-haired twat with big red plastic glasses and a big floppy red bow-tie.

I cannot; I will not allow my people to suffer like this.

I take my place at the crowded bar, and wait – and three songs in, the moment presents itself. After setting up some bastard to rape and pillage a classic sixties ballad, the karaoke twat slips off to the toilet.

I down my pint.

The karaoke gimp is there at the left-hand stall. He senses me coming in, and flicks his head round to look at me. I walk towards the sinks and I stop, for the slightest hint of a second, right behind him. I don't really stop, I just . . . pause for a tiny half a heartbeat behind him where he can't see me. And the trickle of his piss against the porcelain comes to a stop as he clenches up in fear.

I head on towards the sink, like I'm going to wash my hands. His gaze is fixed dead ahead but his whole attention is focused on me. He stands there, at once shitting himself, and yet, at the same time, cruelly unable to piss.

I rinse my hands under the taps and – it all comes together for me. From the bar I can still hear the chords from his karaoke machine, and I just . . . hum along to them –

He hums 'You've Lost That Loving Feeling'.

'If you feel like a sing-song, you should have a go,' he says.

I stop what I'm doing. I stop with the rinsing my hands under the taps and slowly, slowly turn my head round to look at him.

'Did you just say things to me?' I ask him.

He stands there, grinning desperately. 'I just meant –' he starts, but I'm on my run now and he's not stopping me.

'Did you just say things to me in the *gents* for fuck's sake?'

'I didn't mean anything by it –'

'Jesus Christ,' I say, 'what the fuck is the world coming to? Fucking gaylords trying it on in the gents of my own bastard local, for fuck's sake.'

'Oh . . . ' he goes, 'oh no, I wasn't trying it on, I'm not a gaylord –'

'Well, you obviously fucking are,' I say. He doesn't know quite how to come back to that. So he just says, 'I'm not.'

'No?'

'No,' he goes.

'Well, in that case,' I go, 'how the *fuck* do you explain that?' And I jab at his great big poofy red fucking bow-tie, 'Cause that is just about as gay as you can get.'

'Oh,' he says, with this great big surge of relief, 'that's just my costume. I do the karaoke, see. I'm the karaoke bloke.'

'Right,' I say. 'Right. So tell me, karaoke bloke – what the fuck're you doing here then?'

6. Crazy Gary's Mobile Disco

You can see then, in his eyes, you can see it just beginning to occur to him that there's more going on here than he thought. More, and worse.

'Well, I'm doing the karaoke, aren't I. Here. Tonight.'

'No you're fucking not,' I say.

'Well . . . I am,' he goes.

'No you fucking can't be,' I say, 'cause tonight is Thursday night, and Thursday night, as every fucker knows, is disco night. *My* disco night.'

The dawn breaks over the murky lifeless continent that is his tiny bastard mind.

'Oh,' he says, 'you're the disco guy, are you?'

'That is abso-fuckin-lutely what am I,' I tell him.

'Right,' he says, 'well,' and he takes off his stupid big glasses and inspects them for muck. 'Thing is, mate, it's not up to me, is it? I mean . . . ' and he shrugs like he's letting me in on some super-fucking-obvious fact of life which I am just too retarded to get a grip on, 'if you lose the crowd, you're gonna lose the gig, aren't you?'

He stands there polishing his glasses and shrugging at me. With this look like – here we are, businessmen having a business discussion and it just so happens that he's in the superior position and what can you do about it.

And what I do about it is: I let him get on with it. I let him imagine he can look down on me. I let him pour it out, and I eat it all up. I let all that shit come and settle in my belly. He's telling me how he knows me and Craig'd been doing Thursdays at the Boar's Head for years and he's very sorry but there's no room for sentimentality in show business, is there, and I nod at him, nod at him, eating his shit all up, nodding at him, thinking, oh, you poor fucker you haven't got a clue, you poor fucker, cause all this shit, it's gonna have to come out, cause that's not gonna sit there in my belly, I'm not gonna let that all melt in my guts and spread out all over me and be carried off and built into my skin and my muscles and my bones, oh no. That bad shit is going to have to come out of me and into someone else, and it looks like that someone else is gonna be you, you poor fucker –

So he puts his glasses back on and straightens his jacket and even extends his hand towards me, and says 'No hard feelings then?'

I step towards him.

And I reach out, like I'm reaching for his hand, and then I grab his head, I grab a handful of his hair, and I slam his face down into the porcelain, so hard that it bangs and bounces straight off, so fast that his head is back where it started before he even realises what's happened, and the only evidence that anything has happened is the sudden burning sensation in his forehead and the absence of his glasses, which have fallen off his face into the sink.

'What did you do that for?' he goes, scrabbling around for his specs.

'You are fuckin with my disco,' I tell him. 'Anyone who fucks with my disco, dies.'

'You wouldn't,' he says, 'you wouldn't dare.'

'Wouldn't I?' I say. 'There's a bloke, a mate of mine. And right now he's exploring the crumbling A-roads of this sinking island, looking for a brand new place to call his home. And you know why?'

The karaoke twat shakes his head. As he must.

'Because,' I tell him, 'because he knows that if he ever comes back here, I'm going to take his fucking face off. And he was a mate. He was like – a brother to me. But he fucked with my disco.'

The karaoke twat steps back into the corner of the room, blinking and making this little mewling noise. I go after him.

'Do your eyes give you trouble?' I ask him. 'Do you find short-sightedness is a problem for you?'

I step towards him and he backs off into the corner.

'Do you, for example, find yourself waving to complete strangers on the street, thinking you know them? And do you not recognise your friends, even when they're stood right in front of you? Does that happen? Does that happen a lot?'

I'm inches from his face now.

'That must make you feel like a right twat. And that probably explains why you look like such a twat, and act like such a twat.'

I reach out, with my finger and thumb, and I gently just close his eyelids. He's shaking. He's actually shaking but he stands there not daring to open his eyes.

'I can bring all that to an end for you,' I tell him. 'Poor sight need never trouble you again.'

He folds up, sinks down on to the floor and hugs himself, eyes closed and shaking and he just whispers, 'Please don't. Please don't. Please don't . . . '

Beat.

I have to leave at that point. Cause he does this thing. This thing which means that either I have to just leave, or I have to –

I'm not even back at the bar when the plug gets pulled on the outro of the classic sixties ballad.

I kick off another pint, and watch the karaoke twat as he dismantles his equipment and scuttles off, never daring to meet my eye.

So it's mission totally accomplished. Thursday nights at the Boar's Head are mine again.

– Just to my left, just next to me at the bar, there is a spoddy little bastard, and he is ill-advisedly allowing his elbow to knock against mine as he struggles to attract the attention of the bar staff. He's stuck – he's got the bar presence of a fucking . . .

Pauses to consider.

. . . twat, and he's starting to sweat it that he's never going to get served, so he's half-pretending that he's not really trying to, half-carrying on his conversation, 'Well, you see, Miranda, I think when you're brought up in cramped streets and beneath close horizons, it just *is* going to foster a certain . . . narrowness of outlook, but with luck it's a narrowness education and experience can do something to rectify . . .'

I'm thinking: now, do I just deck the cunt straight off?

– or do I go in for a little psychological torture – do I make the spoddy little bastard volunteer for a kicking?

He's with this gang of flat-chested bitches and I could just . . . pick one at random and gently start massaging her arse, slide my hand up her thigh and she'd be there with this look of panic that would never quite leave her face again –

She'd be staring at him, not daring to scream, do something! do something! – and even though he's shiteing it, even though he's pissing himself – he'll have to step up to me –

And then when he does, the question is . . .

. . . to glass, or not to glass?

To glass, I think.

There are those who say that to open by glassing is a cheap, vulgar move, and . . . to those people, I say – I *understand* how you feel. And I'm glad you feel that way. Because it means that if we ever . . . encounter one another, you're gonna end up on your knees, screaming and covered in blood, and I'm gonna be laughing in your fucking face . . . which will be in bits all over the floor.

The spoddy little bastard gives up on ever getting served and turns to lead his crew of skinny-necked freak children – several of whom I know and hate from schooldays – up and out from the pub, apparently on their way to some bijou little gathering with cheese and wine and sun-dried tomatoes on ciabatta and the most mouth-watering olives, simply pitted in green and anchovy-stuffed in black –

And inspiration strikes. If I'm going to kick off with a spoddy little four-eyed bastard, why do it in a public bar, where mine host will think badly of me for disrupting his evening's business, and mine host's door supervisors may well leap on me and prevent me from giving the spoddy little bastard the attention he deserves? Why not do it in the comfort of the spoddy little bastard's home – and have the extra thrill of smashing up his poncy gaff?

So I get Shirl behind the bar to spot me a bottle of voddy, and I join the gang.

'You don't mind if I tag along with you,' I say.

This look passes between them: suddenly we are all back in school. I am the nasty school bully, and they are my gutless, bedwetting victims. For all their BAs and MScs and years out snorting opium and shagging ethnic in India, when you cut to the fucking crap they are still the same friendless twats, shiteing it in the face of the nasty school bully.

This one bitch forces a smile. 'No, Dai, we don't mind at all.'

I force a pained smile back, and I go, 'I'm not Dai. Dai was my brother. Who died.'

And the bitch looks at me like I've just punched her in the stomach – and, who knows, I may well do later on – and I'm in.

The gaff, the party, is a fuckin wreck, obviously – even before I've got to work on the place. It's all crybaby college rock and don't we *all* feel let down by the Assembly but you know I'd go on hunger strike if they tried to take it away from us now . . . I look at these tossers and I thank the Lord I'm part of the disenfranchised non-working class, I really fucking do.

I decide to open by necking every last drop they've got before kicking off with the headbutts, the kidney jabs and the throat stabbings – first insult, then the injuries. It shouldn't be a problem, drinking their pathetic stash dry – what with me being the hardest bloke in town after Harbisher, Woodward and Spanswick, and these gits all being a bunch of fucking pussies. So I move into the kitchen to inspect their bring-a-bottle collection –

Beautiful moment of po-mo epiphany. He comes to a halt.

And there she is. Hovering over the drinks, looking really not at home, knocking back a can of Fosters – in one – and just . . . and just a strand of amber nectar missing her mouth, streaking down her perfect throat . . . and as that little lager drip hits the scoop neck of her white cotton-Lycra-mix bra top, it blossoms, like a little . . . like a teensy-weensy little light-brown mushroom cloud.

He struggles.

And it wasn't even like she was what you'd call conventionally fit. She was major-league fuckable, but more glamour model than catwalk model. German porn more than Scandinavian porn. She was fuckin perfect.

He snaps out of it.

So there I am, in this party full of tossers, five seconds ago just about to kick off and smash the place up, and now all that bad shit in my belly has vanished and I'm just thinking, oh my shiteing Christ, how do I get to fuck this chick?

Normally I'd just be like, 'Wanna drink?', 'Wanna another drink?' and fuckin 'How about it, then?'

But that's how you do it when you've got fifteen chicks lined up against a bar and you don't particularly give a shit what you end up copping off with so long as you cop off with something. This chick, though – with this chick, I've got to get *her*.

It's not like I haven't gone for specific chicks before – like for a bet, or to piss some fucker off by bagging his bitch. What you do is, you just start talking and you ask her about work or if she's going on holiday or whatever, and when she starts rabbiting on first you just look her straight in the eye like you're really fucking riveted, and then after about five minutes you let your gaze slide away over her shoulder, and she gets panicky. She keeps talking but she's really checking out your threads, realising you're a pretty fuckin hip and happening guy and she's just some third-division smalltown minger, and she looks a bit of a twat to be even trying it on with a body so obviously out of her sexual league –

And then you swoop back in, you brush your hand against her arm, and you really quietly tell her someone walked by who was the absolute spit of somebody really close to you who died, and she'll be *so fuckin grateful* you weren't just bored shitless with her and so impressed with what a sensitive motherfucker you are, and she'll start on about some bastard she vaguely knew or perhaps just fucked who died of smack or AIDS or being stabbed in the neck, and as she gets into her story you look away, not over her shoulder this time but down at the floor with this dead-pained expression on your face. She won't notice for a second that you're not really listening, and when it does hit her, when she sees the look on your face she'll reach out and say, what's wrong, what's wrong, and you'll say, look, it's OK, right, it's just . . . it was my brother Dai what died, and he actually died of AIDS or smack or whatever she was talking about – and she'll feel like such complete shit that she'll go down on you right there and then; even if her bastard boyfriend is sitting in the fucking room, that bitch is eating out of your lap, no worries. And if you ever want to shag her again, you can: you just have to be a total cunt to her, and she'll be all – I know there's this sadness in him, if I could just get him to open up to me again, if only . . .

But as I'm watching this perfect chick wipe the Fosters from her chin, I'm thinking – that's not gonna work here.

Cause there was something –

It was just this way she had of looking, see. She –

Christ, I'd say she looked like flowers, but flowers look like shit, really. She looked like –

Like on a really fucking sweltering day, your pits are drenched with just the effort of reaching up to open the front door, and you're dying for a drink but you're fucking broke, so when you pass the pub you try not to look in, cause you're only torturing yourself, but you can't help it. So you look – and you see this crew of little shits sitting by the window and maybe you just laid off kicking them in a couple of weeks ago, and so you wander over and they all start pissing themselves, and they rush to buy you a pint, just to keep on your good side. And you're sitting there with your pint on this sticky table, you reach out and take a good swig, maybe two fingers so maybe an eighth of the pint is gone already, but you've still got seven-eighths of the pint left, and it's a classy pint, something triple-brewed and chill-filtered, and the fizz of it in your throat beats any baking-soda buzz, and it scours every little rotting crevice in your mouth, making your mouth a place where some lager-drinking glamour model might actually want to spend some time, and as the fizz settles down in your stomach you've still got seven-eighths of that pint sitting there, still almost a full pint and just a couple of degrees above zero . . .

A moment like that – it can turn your whole day around.

Beat.

This chick looked like that moment.

I've seen stuff like this before. There's shows about it on the telly. There's a word for it, it's like a condition or a syndrome or something and you get it and all your mates are going, why the fuck don't you come out any more? And you're going, I can't, see I gotta stay in and just hang round this chick cause I got this fucking syndrome, and they go, yeah, fucking boring fucker syndrome, and you're going, no, no it's not that. It's not that it's something –

– else.

So I couldn't just go up and talk all my usual shite, could I? Cause this was just . . . not the usual shite that comes along.

I was stuck. There was this moment, this thing dying to happen, this fucking perfect chick standing right in front of me and I was just standing there like a fuckwit, and eventually, in due fucking course, she was just gonna turn her back or maybe wander out the back for a fag or maybe get totally fucking bored and call a taxi and piss right off and be fucking gone for ever. And I'd be left there knowing it had all been that bastard close and –

The trance breaks.

And then, sal-fuckin-vation. The spoddy little bastard from the pub comes stumbling up to the perfect girl, grabs a bottle of lager, opens it – like a tosser, faffing around with an actual bottle-opener rather than biting the cap off or slamming it against a radiator – and then he – he tries to fucking talk to her.

And I think – you fucking STAR. Who the fuck needs chat-up lines when you've got overwhelming physical superiority on your side?

I saunter up, casual like, and say to the girl, 'Is this fuckwit bothering you, love?' And the spoddy little bastard actually jumps. He's just about to take a swig of beer and his hand freezes, caught halfway to his mouth.

He turns round, the creepy little smile vanishing off his face, and looks at me, not quite believing what's gonna happen to him, babbling, 'I wasn't, I wasn't, I don't want any trouble, I was just *talking to her*, for God's sake.'

'And why the fuck,' I say, 'would a quality chick like this want to talk to a stupid little fuck like you?'

And he just . . .

He gestures – tears on the bastard's cheeks.

The worst that's gonna happen is he's gonna get a mild kicking – and he's just there . . . like a fucking baby in front of this girl. I can't stand for that. So I'm gonna have to leave, which I really don't wanna do, or I'm gonna have to –

What I do is, I grab the bastard's bottle, and make like I'm gonna slam it in his face – but then stop like two inches in front of his nose, so the beer splashes all over him. He's standing, beer dripping down him, looking like a fucking twat, but at least you can't tell he was actually . . .

At least if his eyes are red he can say it was the beer.

He stands there and fidgets and drips. And he looks so pathetic, I'm thinking – piss off, piss off now, or I'm going to find myself doing things to get rid of you, and now is just not the moment for that kind of stuff –

And – thank bastard God – he turns away from me.

And so there I am. Just me and the perfect girl. I'm looking at her, and she's just standing there, looking at me, and one of us is gonna have to say something but neither of us wants to say anything shit, in case it ruins the moment, but at the same time neither of us is walking away or getting embarrassed, we're just . . . waiting.

And finally, she says:

With reverence.

'Cheers for getting rid of that twat for me.'

And it's perfect, isn't it. It's like – not too complicated, not too simple, it's not saying too much, it's just – saying what needs to be said. And we both know what is *actually* being said.

So I'm like, 'Fucking no problem at all, love, any fucking time. I just can't stand to see men being disrespectful to a lady, like, won't fucking stand for it.'

'Well,' she says, 'you're a real gentleman, aren't you?'

'So,' I say, 'what's your name, love.'

'Mary,' she says.

Coming over all dreamy (to the rhythm of 'Mary, Mary Quite Contrary').

. . . Mary. Mary, Mary . . . pretty as a fairy.

Snaps out of it.

'I know what you're thinking,' she says.

'What,' I say.

'You're thinking – fucking *Virgin Mary*, aren't you?'

'No,' I say, 'no, I wasn't thinking that at all. I was just thinking what a lovely name that is.'

'Really?' she goes. 'Cause that's what everyone says – Virgin Mary. Or Virgin on the Ridiculous. Or Bloody Mary, my dad calls me – cause he always says, ten minutes of me and he needs a bloody drink.'

'Does he?' I say, laughing – laughing, and thinking, oh, does he? Remind me to give him a fucking slap next time I see him, he won't be such a fucking comedian then.

'So,' she goes, 'you gonna tell me your name, then, or am I gonna have to fucking guess it or what?'

And then my fucking phone goes and I'm grinning at her and apologising like a fucking twat as I'm trying to remember which pocket the bastard thing's in, and I get it out, and it's fucking Janey, and I'm like, 'Janey, for fuck's sake, what do you fucking want?' and she's all, 'Where you been? What you doing?' So I tell her, 'I been taking care of business. Obviously.'

'Oh,' she says. 'Can you come over? I been all on my own with the babby for ages.'

'No, no, I fucking cannot.'

'But I haven't seen you for days –'

'Actually, Janey,' I say, 'I'm in the fucking middle of something, if you must know, so I gotta go. All right?'

She doesn't say a thing, hoping I won't hang up on her when she's throwing a strop. But I do.

'Now, where was I?' I ask the perfect girl.

'You were just about to tell me your name,' she says.

'Oh yeah,' I say. 'Let me give you my card,' and I whip one out.

' "Crazy Gary's Mobile Disco",' she says, 'is that you, Crazy Gary?'

'Well, yeah,' I say. 'It's a professional name, obviously. I'm not really called Crazy Gary. It used to be "Craig and Gary's Mobile Disco", I used to do it with my brother Craig, but then we fell out, and – he had to leave town. And the van had "Craig and Gary's Mobile Disco" on the side, and I thought, fuck, I'm going to have to get that all resprayed – but then I realised, I could just change the "Craig and" to "Crazy", and then it would say "Crazy Gary's Mobile Disco". And so, Crazy Gary was born.'

'Right,' she says.

'Yeah,' I says. 'I did the respray job myself. I looked at it and thought – fuck you, all the teachers in the world who said I was thick, cause that was a fuckin smart piece of respraying. Plus, fuck you, because you are teachers, who are twats who wank off thinking about schoolgirls in their little navy gym slips: whereas I've got my own fucking disco, and I get to wank off all over schoolgirls in their little navy gym slips, every fucking weekend if I want to.'

'Right,' she says. Just 'right'. Not actually sounding that impressed. Five seconds ago – that smile. And now – nothing.

He racks his brains.

It was the stuff about wanking off over underage girls, wasn't it. Cause loads of chicks find that sort of stuff a little bit . . . they just don't really dig it *that much*.

So I tell her: 'Look, what I said just now, about wanking over chicks in school uniform. I don't really do that. I think it's sick, it's fucking disgusting. And I've never been with an underage girl. Except obviously a couple of times when I've been pissed, but they've always *looked* old enough to be legal.'

'Who hasn't made that mistake,' she says. 'And as it happens, I think dressing up is laugh. I've kept all my school uniforms specifically for, you know – sex games, basically.'

His eyes widen . . .

'Really . . . '

'Oh yeah,' she says. 'I think it's dead sad when people can't explore and express the really filthy, depraved, extreme sides of their personalities within a consensual sexual relationship. It makes for crap shagging, for starters.'

He swallows hard. It takes him a moment to come to terms with this . . .

'Well, yeah,' I say. 'I'm just the same.'

This chick really is it. I don't even have to bullshit her about all my little perversions – she's . . . *just like me*, for fuck's sake.

Beat.

And I'd be fucked off if she was blabbering away on the phone to some other fucker while I was trying to crack on to her, for fuck's sake –

'That was Janey on the phone,' I tell her. 'She's like – my sister-in-law. She wanted to see if I could come over and – babysit.'

'Oh, yeah?' Mary says.

'Yeah,' I say. 'I mean, I fucking love her kid – I'm fucking great with kids, by the way – but Jane, she like – she never *thinks*, you know, phones me all hours telling me the kid's done this or the kid's done that, or wanting me to come over. Never thinks, like, that I might have other things to do. I'm not like, shagging her or anything.'

'Right,' is all she says. And still no smile. Doesn't she fucking – believe me? Does she think I'm fucking lying to her?

And I say, 'It's just, you looked a bit, you know, not that impressed. I gave you my card and usually chicks are impressed I've got me own business, and you weren't, so I thought – fuck. What've I done? So I put two and two together, and thought maybe you were getting a bit jealous, like, of me talking to some other bitch while I'm chatting you up.'

And she says, 'No, it wasn't that. It was just – I thought I recognised you, off the telly. I thought you were that rugby player, whassisname.'

He's taken down a peg or two.

'Yeah, yeah, a lot of people do say that. I do look like him. And I did used to play, when I was a kid.

'I don't really like to talk about it but . . . when I was a kid, they thought I was gonna be the saviour of Wales. But I got this groin strain just before a match, Wales Under-18s v. England Under-18s, at the Arms Park. I couldn't let the boys down, obviously, so I went on, scored the try that won us the match ten seconds before the whistle. And my groin was permanently fucked. I had to give up the game that could've made me a bastard household name.'

'For real?' she says.

'Hey,' I says, 'do I look like the kind of bloke who'd lie just to impress a chick?'

'Well, fuck me,' she says. 'That's really fucking tragic.'

'Yeah, I know,' I say. 'You see the state of Wales now, they could've fucking done with me.'

'No,' she says, 'I mean you.' And she steps towards me, and just puts her hand lightly on my arm . . .

'If only I'd been there. I do, like, massage and stuff,' and she brings her face very, very near to mine, and whispers, 'I could've sorted your groin out for you.'

And when she says it, I mean, it's like a come-on – fair enough, obviously it's a fucking come-on – but it's not *just* a come-on, you know?

She like – actually fucking means it.

She says, 'So, no, I wasn't jealous of Jane. Because . . . Jane's not going home with you tonight, is she?'

She steps back, necks the rest of her can, and smiles at me. 'Right,' she says, 'I'm just off to the toilet to freshen up,' she says. 'Don't go anywhere.'

And I wanna come back with some dead snappy line like, 'I won't go anywhere, lovely, cause I can't, cause I can't fucking walk, cause I've got a hard-on the size of a fucking fire-extinguisher.'

But I don't.

I just blink.

I just blink, cause I've got some grit or something in my eye, and it's making them water.

'Fucking typical,' I say, 'a moment like this. And I get something in my eye, for fuck's sake.'

'Yeah,' she says, 'fucking typical,' and she goes off to the toilet.

So I'm standing there like blinking and wiping my eyes for I don't know how long, just people bumping into me – I say people, I mean fucking tossers, of course – and usually I'd like bump them back, but I just stand there.

And finally as she comes out of the toilet, she's walking back towards me and this ugly little bastard comes up to her, this shortarsed little shitehawk comes up to her, and he actually grabs her, and I think, I *should* put that fucker through the window and then go outside and stamp on his fucking face till there's nothing left of him – but I just feel sort of sorry for the poor bastard. He's one of these wide-eyed kids who's fucking terrified of the world and specifically the way it has people like me in it. One of these kids you look at him and you have to look twice to see he really is a kid, cause he already has the slump and the paunch and the permanently robbed look of the fat middle-aged fucker he's gonna wake up one day and discover he's become.

And I just think – you tragic little twat. I pulled the perfect girl, and there you are, you can see her, you can smell her deodorant, you can even touch her arm –

But you're never gonna fuck her. What must it be like, to be such a fucking gimp, and see perfection, and know you're too much of a shitehawk to ever have it?

My phone goes again.

'Janey, what the fuck do you want?'

And she's all, 'Can't you come over, I get so lonely just me and the kid. You don't know what it's like, never getting to talk to a grown-up all day.'

I start to lose my temper with her.

'For fuck's sake, Jane, I'm –'

He turns.

'– I'm doing a fucking deal here, for fuck's sake, and it's not fucking helping having you make me look like some pussywhipped little shit, all right?'

And she's all moany, about to cry, all, 'I'm sorry I ever started this now. I wish Craig was still here. If he came back tomorrow I'd tell him everything and then you'd be fucking for it. He'd fucking have you then. He'd smash your fucking head in if he knew about us.'

'No,' I tell her. 'I don't think he would, Janey. Do you wanna know what I think he'd do? I think he'd just stand there, with this awful look on his face, blinking like a twat and asking why you'd done it to him. And you think you're sorry now – well if you saw him like that, and he was asking you why, and there was nothing you could say to explain it to him, just things you could do to make him shut up – then you'd know what sorry was, you dull fucking bitch.'

And she's got nothing to say to that: so I put the phone down on her.

He turns back.

And she's gone. Mary's gone.

I run round the fucking party, and she's nowhere. I grab the spoddy little bastard.

'Where's that girl,' I say, 'and don't say what girl, or I'll fucking put you through that fucking wall.'

And he goes, 'She left.'

'What?'

He starts whimpering.

'She left. With that guy she was just talking to.'

I punch him, obviously. 'No she fucking didn't.'

'OK then,' he goes, 'she didn't.'

I punch him again, and because he's wailing by now I cut my fucking hand on his nasty little teeth, and that really pisses me off, and he's just going 'I'm sorry, I'm sorry,' so I butt the bastard and let him drop to the floor.

On the street, there's no one. MARY! I'm actually screaming MARY! Cause I can see all this stuff, all this Hollywood shit, and it's all slipping away from me. MARY! MARY! I run down the fucking street, I can't see her. I run back the other way – there's no one there. I lose it, I run just down fucking alleys not knowing where I am, screaming MARY, MARY and my fucking legs are giving out, and I'm thinking, gotta keep running, gotta fucking find her, just this once don't fuck it up, don't fuck it up this time, please don't fuck it up –

But my fucking legs are fucking killing me and it hurts like fuck to breathe, but I'm going, gotta keep running, gotta find her –

And though I'm thinking gotta keep running, I'm not running, I'm not running at all, I'm on my knees, I'm collapsed, I'm chucking up from the effort, and I've fucking fucked it up again, I've let her get away, I've fucked it up. I've fucked it up again.

And I'm on my knees, slumped against a wall.

And I don't know what I'm doing. I'm shaking. And I can't breathe. And I put my hands to my face and when I take them away again they're wet. And I don't know what I'm doing here.

And I think, but of fucking course. Of course this is how it works out. She just fucking vanishes off the face of the earth. What the fuck else do you expect?

What the fuck else do you expect, when you got all this bad stuff, all this bad stuff growing in your belly. That's not just gonna go away, is it? That's there for ever. Nothing's gonna get rid of that. And you are a fucking twat if you think any little bitch is going to get rid of that.

I rub my eyes.

In the shadows, over the road, I see –

I see that shortarsed fucking shitehawk who took her away from me. And it occurs to me, I should drag myself to my feet and get on over there and fuck him up.

But what's the fucking point of that? What the fuck will that even *do*? The bitch is gone, as if a fucking bitch could do anything.

And so I close my eyes –

And when I open them I'm on the other side of the road and I've picked him up and slammed him against the wall and I'm screaming at him, and I'm gonna take his fucking face off, I'm gonna castrate the fucking bastard – and I can see he's screaming but I can't hear it, I can't hear nothing –

And I blink, and when I open my eyes, I've let the fucker go, and he falls. He falls straight to the floor, doesn't even try and stay up. And –

He's down there on the floor, on his knees, scrabbling around, and I can't hear a thing but I can see, he's like he's begging me, he's begging and pleading and going 'Please don't, please don't, why, why, why've you done this? And I don't wanna hear it so I'm screaming over it, screaming at him:

'You think you've got her, you little shitehawk, you think you've got her off me, well, you think about this: everything you've ever wanted to do to her but've never had the nerve, I'm gonna find her and do it to her tonight.'

And even then, *even then*, he doesn't try and get up and smack me one, he just lies there squirming, and I can't bear it and I see how if I just bring my boot down on that face, it'll bring that all to an end, and so I wait for just a moment for his vision to clear, so he'll understand what I'm doing to him isn't an accident, it's a very deliberate response to that awful broken look on his face which is more than I can put up with –

And my phone goes.

'Janey,' I say, watching his eyes crack open, 'I'll be round to sort things later but I've just gotta finish something right now –'

And she says, 'Sorry to disappoint, but it's not Janey.'

Beat.

'What the fuck d'you want,' I say to her.

'I knew it,' she says.

'What?' I say.

'Fucking typical,' she says. 'I knew you'd be like this.'

'Well, what the fuck d'you expect,' I says to her. 'One moment we're chatting and getting on nicely, the next – you've fucked off for no reason.'

'I fucked off for no reason. That's what happened, is it?' she says.

'Well, yeah.'

'Cause let me tell you what happened from where I was standing,' she says. 'From where I was standing, we were talking.'

'Right.'

'But the talking wasn't what it was about.'

Gary *says nothing. She goes on.*

'Cause underneath the talking, I was thinking – fuck me, something's happening here.'

Gary *says nothing. She goes on.*

'Something pretty fucking massive. But I wasn't sure, cause when can you ever be sure about other people.'

Gary *says nothing.*

'So I wasn't sure, till you told me this really tragic story about your groin getting fucked up and I said I wished I could've been there to help you –'

'Yeah,' I says to her, 'and then you changed your mind, didn't you.'

'You fucker,' she says. 'I wasn't sure, cause you never can be, and then you told me about your groin getting fucked up and then I said I wished I could have been there – and then what happened?' she says.

'I got some grit in my eye,' I tell her.

Beat.

'Well, tara then, Gary.'

'Don't go –' I says to her.

'It's been really fucking disappointing getting to know you –'

'OK,' I says to her.

'What?' she says.

'I didn't have no grit in my eye,' I says to her.

'Well, what then,' she says.

'They just filled up, didn't they.'

'With what?' she says to me.

'With water,' I says.

'With what?' she says.

'With tears,' I tell her.

Beat.

''Right then,' she says. 'In that case, I don't think we need to waste any more time, do we?'

'No,' I says.

'Get down the Boar's, and give's a call when you get there. I'll come and meet you.'

He puts his phone away.

The kid is still crying to himself on the floor. I go over to check he's all right and he thinks I'm gonna have another go cause he curls himself up. And starts crying again.

I just stand there and take it as he screams and sobs at me. I take it all in. I try to take, but it all goes straight through, it doesn't touch me.

And there's nothing in me – not a single tremor, not the hint of reflex spasm – that wants to grind his face into the floor.

And all the bad shit in my belly, that's just gone, it's like it belonged to someone else entirely, some poor sod who's gonna spend his whole life prowling around the streets kicking, and cutting, and stabbing, and never realising that the more he kicks and the more he cuts, the more bad shit there is coming after him. Never realising – until the day the shit catches up with him, and finally he has to pay.

That poor sod isn't gonna be me. I'm getting off the streets right fucking now. There's just seconds to go. Seconds from now, and I'm going to be home, and safe, in the arms of the perfect girl.

2: a righteous brother

Mathew D. Melody *swaggers on stage, occasionally spraying his throat from a little water bottle to keep it nice and moist.*

Tonight **Mathew** *is wearing a charity-shop dinner suit with a preposterous ruffle shirt, and a bow-tie undone around his neck.*

A tense man – an executive, a vice-president – arrives home from work. As his sports car pulls into the drive, his wife looks up from her gin and weekly magazine, and sighs. She stands, walks upstairs and changes to go out. She dresses absent-mindedly, as if she no longer cares for how she looks, as if she were a lowly waitress at a dimestore diner throwing on a faded uniform – and yet she's putting on a thousand-dollar dress, and a string of the finest pearls. Meanwhile, her husband broods in the conservatory, nursing a Scotch on the rocks. He hears his wife's footfalls on the stair, and stalks back out to the car. Only after she slams her own door shut, only after he fires up the powerful engine, does he turn and leave a kiss on her cheek.

They drive to their country club and are shown to their customary seats in the cocktail lounge. The drinks arrive – pink gin and the driest of martinis – and it's then that I take the stage.

I look at them, and I see: a woman so exquisite she can bear no ornament beyond her simple string of pearls, with an elegant, noble man in a crisply tailored suit. I see a modern tragedy unfolding before my eyes. I see a sweet young boy and –

– the perfect girl, and I see . . . that they have forgotten they are in love.

I greet the crowd, nod to the band-leader, and as the band strikes up, a love song – something simple and classic – I close my eyes . . .

. . . and I cut out a little of my heart, and give it up to that . . . exquisite lady. As I sing, she forgets the drink, the club, even the man she came in with: there's just she and I, walking on a distant tropical beach at sunset, as I sing for

her. The balmy air fills her lungs, she hears the rustle of the
sea breeze through the palms . . .

. . . and she feels love again, as fresh as when it was first
love. She feels love again, as if it *were* first love.

The music ends; I bring her gently back to earth. She wakes
from the song, light-headed, dizzy with shock, and . . . she
looks into the eyes of her husband. She looks into his eyes,
still drunk on the scent of that tropical night, and she falls in
love with him all over again. And she forgets I even exist.

That piece of my heart which belongs for ever to that
exquisite lady breaks, as before my eyes, they melt into one
another.

He gulps back the lump in his throat.

I do that. I make that happen with a song. I strip away the
greyness, the deadness, and I sing love back to life. I know
your world is drained of colour and glamour, but try to
imagine mine. Try to imagine that joy.

I finish my tale. The young woman who could have been a
beauty sits back and regards me coldly. She says:

'Well, that's as may be, Mr Melody, but the fact remains –
you've been unemployed for twenty-four months and you
haven't found work as a professional cabaret singer. Now,
there are some store assistant positions become available at
Tesco's – can I get you an application?'

I say to her, 'No. You cannot.'

She says, 'Well, I think you really should consider it,
because these positions require no previous experience nor
qualifications. I can arrange an interview for this afternoon;
you could be on the shopfloor this evening stacking away
and tonight you can be out having a drink with the boys to
celebrate your brand new job.'

'That's no good,' I tell her. 'I shall be rehearsing all
afternoon for a very important showbusiness engagement

this evening, after which I will be taking my beloved Candy to dinner.'

She scowls at me. 'If you won't even apply for a job which you could in fact do, Mr Melody, then it's clear you're not really seeking employment at all. And then it's my duty to tell you that while I don't make the law, I do enforce it, and so I'll have to be putting a stop to your benefits.'

I say: 'Look, Ms –'

And I want to call her by her name, because she's been handling mine rather roughly throughout this whole conversation, but I can't quite read it because the print on her badge is very small –

'Look, Ms, what you must understand is that I have something infinitely more valuable than shelf-stacking to offer the world. If I spent my life stacking shelves for Mr Tesco or Mr Safeway, I would go mad. My downstairs neighbour, for example, she stacks shelves for Mr Tesco, and she's quite ga-ga. You can't force me to take a job that's dangerous to my mental health.'

'Threats to your mental health are of no interest to the law,' she says. 'If you actually go mad – well, that's a different matter. But the law will not be held hostage to your threats.'

'But that's not fair,' I tell her.

'It may in your opinion be,' she says, 'but ours is not to reason why, is it, Mr Melody.'

'Well, it occurs to me that our ancestors fought and died in two world wars to make sure that it was ours to reason why, as it happens, Ms –'

And I lean across the desk to peer at her name badge, but the print's so small I have to – squint and screw my eyes up to make out what it says – Ms . . . Bunstable? Barnstable? Bunion? Bungle?

And she screams at me!

'Will you stop staring at my breast!' she screams.

Except she doesn't use the word 'breast'. She uses a word rather coarser than that.

For a second I am too stunned to speak.

Me – as if – I would never stare at a lady's – never! I mean – what would my mother say –

I reach out over the desk, just meaning to comfort her – and she jumps back, knocking her chair over.

'Don't you dare lay your filthy fingers on me,' she says, except she doesn't use the word 'filthy'.

'I'm sorry,' I tell her. 'I'm so sorry, but I really didn't do anything wrong, you know. I didn't.'

One of the lady's fellow workers comes over, a big man, and he grabs me, without listening to a word I have to say on the matter. He carries me out of the office and deposits me none too gently on the pavement.

It's at times like this I feel like giving in. Sitting in a puddle on the pavement, kids whizzing past me on all sorts of boards and blades, all of them laughing, none of them stopping to help . . . red and wet and cold, and all on what's supposed to be the most important day of my life so far. How would I feel – if my beloved Candy saw me now, how would I ever live down the shame?

I pick myself up. Through the window of the Job Centre I can see the lady, with people crowding round her, comforting her. I tap on the window to try and apologise.

Mimes as he speaks.

I didn't mean to stare

Points to his eyes.

at your breast,

Cups his hands in front of his chest.

all right?

Then gives a thumbs-up.

But the nasty man starts to come outside again, and I scarper.

As I'm running, I remember what my mum says – to understand all is to forgive all. So what I do is, I go to a newsagent's and buy a nice card with flowers on the front, to try and explain.

Dear Job Centre Lady,

I really didn't mean to stare at your . . . chest today. If I seemed like I was being a little bit odd, well, my doctor did say I might be, and I know I was late coming to sign on, because I overslept, but I hardly got a wink of sleep last night.

First, that lady from downstairs – the one who's ga-ga, cause she has to stack shelves – her cat was scratching at my door. I shouted at it to go, but it just wouldn't. It went on and on, scratching and mewling, and finally I'd had all I could take. I took the chain off, opened the door, and said to her: look, little cat, if you don't lay off scratching my door, I'm going to lose my temper with you – and then there'll be no telling what I'll do.

It stared me in the eye, as if it was thinking about answering back – but then thought better of it, and went prowling off down the corridor.

I got back into bed, and counted Frank Sinatra songs with the word 'love' in the title, and as I finally got to nodding off –

There's them next door. Rowing again.

I say it's them rowing, but of course it's not a them you hear. It's a her. Her, screaming and slamming and throwing.

And fair enough, it's not that loud. Fair enough, it's not like I couldn't put the radio on to cover it up but it's not just the sound, you see.

It's the knowing.

The knowing that just in the next building there's this couple. Tearing each other's hearts to pieces.

The noise I could ignore. But the *tragedy* . . .

I buzz at their front door. There are footfalls on the stairs, and the door opens.

'It's just,' I say, 'I've got an awful lot on tomorrow, I wouldn't dare to intrude normally.'

She stares at me.

'It can't be doing you any good,' I say, 'shouting at each other like that.'

'I shout at him,' she says, 'because he peeves me off.' Except she doesn't say 'peeves'.

'Well, have you ever thought,' I say, 'that he might have an awful lot going on. In his mind. And if you tried to see things from his point of view, you might understand him better, and then you might not argue so much.'

She stares at me some more; and then her frown breaks.

'You know you're right,' she says. 'I'll do that; and you know, he'd be really touched by you thinking about us. Why don't you come on up and tell him what you've just told me.'

He almost wants to; pulls back.

'Best not,' I tell her. 'But I've brought you this little pamphlet, it's got Bible stories in it and there are some parables on page seven about judging not lest ye be judged and putting yourself in the other man's shoes that might be of interest to you –'

'Oh, go on, come up,' she says. 'See, the thing is, we argue because afterwards we get to make up. And how we make up, is –'

Back in my room I try and say a prayer for them: that the parables will do the trick and whatever is tormenting them and troubling them is fixed soon, and ideally within the next twenty-four hours, as I don't want to have to go through another night of banging and crashing next door – but try as I might I can't concentrate on praying because –

Because the scratching starts again!

I get up, open the door, and the cat is there, peering up at me.

I speak to it in the strongest tones I can muster. 'That's it,' I tell her. 'I've had about enough. You'd better leave me in peace – or I'm going to go downstairs and get your mother up and tell her how naughty you're being – and I don't think she'll be very happy being woken up at this time of night, do you?'

But this cat – looking me right in the eye – she raises her paw –

and then lashes out, and drags her claws right across my shin –

and I kick out.

I kick out, and send her flying.

She hits the wall, and – you know how they say cats always land on their feet? Well, she doesn't. She just hits the wall, and . . . sort of slides down it, and then . . . hits the floor.

I'm not normally like that at all, I'm normally the most placid person you could hope to meet, or so my mum says, but the doctor did tell me that I might be a bit short-tempered for a while.

'Well,' I say to the cat. 'That's what you get, isn't it.'

She doesn't move. 'I said, that's what you get for scratching, isn't it.'

I go over to her. She's breathing, but she isn't moving . . . and there's . . . there's this little string of blood out of the side of her mouth.

'You'd best go home now, little cat,' I tell her.

But the blummin thing just wouldn't move.

So, I got a cushion, and put her on it, and brought her into the flat. I put a little saucer of milk by the side of the cushion, but it didn't seem to spark her interest, so I put a tea towel over her as a blanket, and went back to bed.

But even then I couldn't sleep cause as she was breathing, the cat was making this wet noise, like she was gargling TCP, and it gave me the creeps.

And so, finally, at about five in the morning, just as dawn was starting to break, I managed to get off to sleep.

And then I overslept, of course, but – as I think you'll agree, Job Centre Lady – it was not really my fault, and so you cannot really blame me for being late to sign on today. It wasn't really my fault, as I hope you'll agree.

I had to buy a pretty big card to get all that on, I can tell you. And I close by saying:

And I'm sorry I was staring at your . . . chest today, only I wasn't, it's just I really wanted to know your name and you'd put your name badge on your chest, so where else was I supposed to look? Best Wishes, Mathew D. Melody.

With that nasty business out the way, all I have to do is check on the Ga-ga Tesco Lady's cat, maybe give her another nourishing saucer of milk and then return her safely to her mummy. And then I'll be set. My accounts will be clear.

I step outside the newsagent's – and a car drives past me at speed and splashes a puddle all over me and soaks me to the skin. A big, nasty car, which pulls up a few yards in front of me. I don't know the name of the model of the car because I've no interest in nasty cars driven by blummin *drugs dealers* – but I do know who it belongs to. Daniel Blister. Daniel blummin Blister. Who sits there looking at me in his rear-view mirror, and laughs, and then once he's sure I've seen him laughing at me, he takes off.

Daniel Blister is not my best friend. Daniel Blister is a childish little pranny.

Daniel Blister was going out with my beloved Candy when she met me and we fell in love.

I was sitting in a pub one night, having a quiet drink on my own at the end of the bar. There was this rowdy group, a stag party, on the other side, and this what I took to be a stripogram came in. But it turned out not to be a stripogram. It turned out to be Candy, doing singing telegrams. She struck up the old Righteous Brothers classic, 'You've Lost That Loving Feeling', and she had the most beautiful voice, I couldn't help but sit up and take note. But she had a cold or a dose of flu – her voice was straining and cracking, and in the end, it just gave out. And all these . . . yobboes were just laughing at her. And I found myself on my feet, walking towards them. I remember them looking at me, getting up like they thought I was going to invite them to step outside. Before I knew what I was doing, I'd picked up the song where she left off. I sang the song for her. And of course, they laughed. They laughed, but I kept on singing,

Sings the chorus to 'You've Lost That Loving Feeling'.

I finished the song, and they were still laughing – so I sang it again.

Sings the first line.

And they laughed again. So I kept singing –

Sings the second line.

One by one, the yobboes fell silent. They ran out of laughter, long before I ran out of song. I had the whole pub, under my spell.

After that, Candy asked me out for a drink to say thanks. And we just talked for hours. I told her about my singing, my gift, and I could tell she was impressed. We were both a bit nervous of each other that night, I think, cause we knew it was something special. She didn't offer me her number - she explained later she just hadn't wanted to look forward – and so I gave her mine. And then . . .

. . . And then it was a couple of weeks before she phoned me. She'd been seeing this guy – this Daniel Blister – and she knew she had to leave him the second she laid eyes on me, she just . . . wanted to give him time to come to terms with the loss, like.

And Candy and I've been seeing each other since then, once a week, every week, without fail. And that's –

Counts.

That's six weeks now. Every Thursday night. I don't see her a lot apart from that because she's got work and all, but we've *kissed* and everything, even though Candy's not the type of girl that really believes in kissing and stuff before marriage. She just says with me she can't help herself. And she has vowed, once we are married . . .

. . . We'll learn all the secrets of physical love together.

And I suppose it's just been really hard for Blister to come to terms with, because, you know, he's had to accept that Candy wasn't really in love with him like she's in love with me. Not at all. *Ever.*

But still: that doesn't excuse him being a childish pranny and a drugs dealer, does it.

So I walk home. Soaked to the skin when I start walking and soaked to the bone by the time I get there.

Outside my building there's a postbox. As I pop the
explanatory note for the Job Centre Lady into it, I say a
little prayer. I say,

Dear Lord God, Sorry about this morning an' all, but I have
now made amends and I hope You will now accept my
accounts are clear cause it is a big day for me and I know I
haven't got a chance in heck unless You and all Your glory
is on my side. Lots of love, for ever and ever, Amen,
Mathew D. Melody.

And that's it. I'm set.

I open the door to my building –

– And I am hit by a flappy, wailing creature.

'Mathew, Matty-Matty-Matty, where've you been?'

It's the Ga-ga Tesco Lady from downstairs – and Nick
Weake, the warden.

'Mathew,' he says, 'I think we have a little problem-ette that
you might be able to solve.'

The Ga-ga Tesco Lady pipes up:

'Matty, Matty, my little catty has gone away! I can't find my
little catty!'

'Yes,' Weake says. 'You know cats, Mathew. They like to
get amongst the pigeons, and occasionally bite the pigeons'
head off.

'Wendy's cat?' I say, and even though I know it's a sin to lie,
I say, 'No, as it happens . . . no. No, Mr Weake, I haven't
seen Wendy's cat for weeks.'

'Well, that's very interesting,' says Weake, 'because Wendy's
been doing a bit of detective work, and she says she detects
fresh cat hairs outside your door.'

The Ga-ga Tesco Lady nods at me emphatically.

'*Fresh* cat hairs,' I say. 'Well, perhaps we'd best take a look. You never know, cats: they sneak around all sorts of places, don't they.'

As I open the door to my flat I say a little prayer to the Lord God to help me think of an excuse, but He doesn't help at all. And of course He wouldn't, cause now I've told a lie, so He's going to be in a mood with me again. The door swings open and Weake pushes past me with the Ga-ga Tesco Lady hot on his heels.

I wait for the inevitable.

Weake marches up, looking sternly at me.

'I'm sorry,' I begin. 'I can't really explain. The doctor said I might be a bit odd but I know that's no excuse –' And Weake cuts me off.

'It seems . . . I owe you an apology,' he says, like the words cause him actual physical pain. 'It seems the cat is not in your room.'

I go in and – the cat's vanished. The Ga-ga Tesco Lady's starting to cry.

'Don't worry, Wendy,' I tell her. 'Your cat's probably just gone exploring. Cats do that.'

'Exactly,' says Weake. 'Wendy, your cat has just gone a-wander. OK? Cats go a-wander. They're hunters. They walk alone. If you can't accept that and handle it in a stable way, well, I'm going to have to recommend you're forbidden to keep pets in future.'

Wendy nods and tries to force a smile – but it's the kind of smile you smile though your heart is breaking; and they're the most heart-breaking smiles of all. And I can only think two things.

First, that I have noticed a big, dark-brown stain on the carpet, just where the cushion with Wendy's cat had been. Or maybe it's . . . more a dark-red sort of a stain.

And the second thing is this: whatever has happened to Wendy's cat, it's going to be Mathew D. Melody's stupid fault. I owe this little lady.

'Wendy,' I say to her, 'Wendy, I'm very sorry about your cat. Is there anything I can do for you to cheer you up till you find her?'

And Wendy's face fills up with a smile. She points at my stereo.

'Karaoke!' she screams.

'Karaoke,' I say.

She nods again.

Of course, if I give her my stereo, I won't be able to rehearse for tonight.

Beat.

But, if I don't make it up to her for kicking her cat then my accounts won't be clear and what's the good of rehearsing if you haven't got the Lord God and all His glory on your side?

'Go on then, Wendy,' I tell her. 'You can have the stereo.'

And she grabs the stereo, and runs off.

Weake shouts after her, but she isn't listening. He turns to me. 'You stay there,' he tells me. 'I've got a bone to pick with you. I'll be back in precisely sixty seconds.'

I shut the door behind him and look around the room.

My suit is no longer laid out neatly on my bed, as I left it.

Somehow, it seems to have moved itself under the bed. One of the sequinned arms of my jacket is protruding slightly from underneath.

I get down on my knees and I see that my suit has somehow rolled itself up into a ball.

It's rolled up in a ball on the floor.

I pull gently on the arm, and drag the ball out from under the bed.

I poke at it. It smells – bad.

I unfold the ball, and – the cat falls out onto the floor. It's not moving, and – it seems to have vomited –

There are all these –

– these red tubes coming out of the cat's mouth tied up with the ruffles on my shirt –

I suspect the cat may be dead.

I hear the door to the Ga-ga Lady's flat slam, and feet on the stairs coming back up to my flat.

I . . . gather the cat up in my costume and run out of the flat.

'Mathew!' Weake shouts up the stairs. 'You stay right where you are.'

I duck into the cleaning cupboard and I have to . . . hold the cat and the suit very tight to my chest to get the door closed, and it . . . makes this gurgling noise, and stuff starts to seep out into my hands.

I hear Weake going into my flat.

'Mathew!' he shouts. 'Where the hell are you?'

I hear him walking into my bathroom, and I make a run for it.

I dash down the stairs – Weake hears me. 'Mathew, what the hell are you playing at?'

I run down the stairs, and into the entrance hall. I'm holding the Ga-ga Tesco Lady's cat wrapped in its own guts and my suit, and Nick Weake is coming down the stairs. He's coming down the stairs, he's going to see me and he's going to know, he's going to see it written on my face that I killed the blummin cat. I look around for some means of escape, but there's nothing, nothing, except . . .

Except the postbox outside our building.

The package of suit and cat is much too big to go through the slot, obviously, but . . .

But the cat *is* dead, after all. I mean, it's not going to know, is it? It's not going to suffer . . .

I run outside. There's no one around. I start to shove the balled-up suit into the slot –

And there are these cracking noises, as the little cat's bones give way –

– and blood or something spurts out onto the postbox but I hope no one will notice because the box is red anyway –

– and with a final shove and snapping and spurting the whole lot drops through.

Weake comes into the hall, and sees me, and marches out of the building.

'I told you to stay put, didn't I? Didn't I?'

'Yes, Mr Weake,' I say, 'but what with all the commotion I felt faint and I needed a breath of fresh air. What was the bone you wanted picking, anyway?'

He scowls at me.

'When I tried to gain entrance to your flat, Mathew, to look for Wendy's cat, I found my key didn't fit the lock. Now, I don't need to tell you, Mathew, do I? I mean, I know I never explicitly said it out loud, but you do understand, don't you, that the whole point of this set-up is that I have keys and can gain entrance to tenants' flats at any time – *purely* for your own well-being. For your benefit, Mathew, not for mine. I mean, I know I've never said, "Mathew, you mustn't get a locksmith in here and have him change the locks so I can't get into your flat," I haven't actually said those exact words, but you knew you weren't supposed to, didn't you?'

'I suppose so, Mr Weake. It's just – I don't like people being able to come in without telling me. My mum used to come in without telling me –'

He cuts me off. 'I can see that later we're going to have to have a little parental damage session about this. Book yourself in next week.'

'Yes, Mr Weake, thank you, Mr Weake,' I say.

I'm in a right state now, aren't I. I've given my stereo to the Ga-ga Tesco Lady and so I can't rehearse, and my suit's stuck in the postbox and even if I could get it out it's going to need a thorough dry-cleaning, and I've hardly got time for that. And the poor postman, he's going to open it up and there'll be this mess of black sequinned suit, dress shirt and thoroughly splattered cat. And then all the letters will be covered in blood and gore . . .

Including my explanatory note to the Job Centre Lady. If that gets all messed up then she won't understand and she won't forgive and my accounts won't be clear and –

He boils and snaps.

This is NOT FAIR! I've tried my best to do everything and put everything right and it's all gone wrong.

Right.

That's it.

He gets down on his knees, clasps his hands, and closes his eyes.

Dear Lord God, I want words with You. I know I upset the Job Centre Lady but I did try to tell her everything in my explanatory note and still it's all gone wrong, and I know she hasn't actually had the explanatory card yet and read it and understood everything and forgiven everything – but it's not my fault if the post takes a whole day, is it?

He waits: then opens his eyes.

My mum told me, sometimes when you pray, all the little noises of the world put themselves together to make a little song . . . and that little song is the voice of the Dear Lord God.

He closes his eyes again, and listens intently for a while.

And there it is!

He sings in a priestly chant.

'Mathew, you didn't tell the Job Centre Lady the whole truth in your explanatory note, did you?'

What d'You mean, Lord. I did . . .

'You didn't tell her the real reason why you were late.'

Well . . .

He opens his eyes; bites his lip guiltily.

I suppose I didn't, no . . .

'And that's why I let the note get all messed up, so you'd have another chance. And I hope you'll tell the whole truth and nothing but the truth this time.'

He leaps to his feet.

Right. Fine. I run across the street to the all-nite Spar and buy another card – even *bigger* this time – and I tell the Job Centre Lady the whole truth.

I wasn't just late because I overslept. The thing was, after I went to the doctor's, I was so proud I –

– I mean I know I shouldn't've, but –

– I was so proud I had to tell somebody, and who else to tell but for Candy, and so – I went round to Candy's place.

I pressed the bell but no one came for ages and ages. I was just about to give up when the door opened – and it was Candy. All glowing and bright and beautiful as ever.

'Candy,' I said, 'thank goodness you're in –'

And she cut me off. 'Mathew,' she said, 'what've we agreed?'

'I know, Candy, I know, but I've just been to the doctor's and he says I'm doing really well and so –'

And she cuts me off again. 'Well, that is good news,' she says. 'But you've spoilt it now, haven't you, coming here. I mean, here I am, spending the whole day –'

And a man walks by the door. In a dressing gown. And as he passes, he says to Candy, 'Cup of tea, love?'

Candy turns and goes, 'Yeah, it's in the cupboard above the sink. Two sugars in mine, please.'

Then she turns back to me.

'Here I am, spending the whole day making myself beautiful for you, and now you've spoilt it.'

'Sorry,' I say.

'Well, sorry's not good enough,' she says. 'I mean, I've got Jamie here . . . giving me shiatsu.'

'Oh, is that what he's doing,' I say.

'Yes,' she says. 'You may like me in them stilettos but they play havoc with my back. Every time I wear them for you, I have to get Jamie round to sort out my spine for me.'

'I'm really, really sorry,' I say.

'Just remember, Mathew: I'm a twenty-first-century woman. I need my space. If you can't accept that, then . . . '

And she slams the door in my face.

Well, after that, I couldn't really face anything. I went for a walk in the park. Then I bought myself a quarter of jelly babies and a bottle of Coke to cheer myself up. And even after I'd drunk it I was still in a moody . . .

. . . In such a moody I just dropped the empty bottle on the pavement, even though I knew full well that it was a crime.

And I carried on walking though I knew I'd done wrong, especially cause it was a glass bottle. I always get them cause I like the feel of them and the weight of them but you have to dispose of them carefully, because they can shatter and have someone's eye, it's the simplest thing. So I started back to try and find the bottle and put it in the bin but then I remembered I was late to come and see you, Job Centre Lady, and that's where it all started to go wrong.

It takes me ages to write all that and by the time I've finished I've only got five minutes to get to the bus stop and catch the bus.

I run over to the postbox, and I'm about to pop in my second explanatory note when I remember – I can't put it in there, cause of the splattered cat! So I run down the street and over the road to the post office, and drop it in there.

And then I run back to the bus stop thinking, that's it, I'm set, I've done everything now, my accounts are all cleared.

Except . . . as I pass the postbox outside my flat, I think: I might have made amends to the Ga-ga Lady for killing her cat, but what about the cat itself?

He comes to a halt.

The bus is due any second – but I go over to the postbox –

Drops to his knees.

– to say a burial prayer for the cat.

> 'Ashes to ashes,
> Funk to funky,
> Hope you enjoy cat heaven,
> And sorry I killed you.
> Lots of love from Mathew D. Melody, Amen.'

He gets up again.

And that's it, that's every last single thing.

I turn – and I see –

The bus.

My bus.

Speeding past the bus stop.

Without me on it.

Falls to his knees again.

No! That is *so* not fair!

And then a car pulls up. It's – Daniel Blister.

He sticks his head out of the window and says, 'Need a lift, mate?'

He gets to his feet in shock.

Well, yeah. I suppose I do.

Thumbs-up to heaven.

Dear Lord God – nice one!

In the car, Daniel Blister – talks to me. He actually says things to me.

'I'm glad I bumped into you,' he says. He looks at me, his mouth hanging open, his tongue worrying at a bit of meat lodged in a crack between his teeth.

'Really?' I say.

'Yeah. I was pissed off when you took me bird off me, sure. And maybe I went round calling you a –'

And he uses a word that begins with 'c', and rhymes with . . . 'unt'.

'– to anyone what'd listen – but I was gutted, wasn't I? What'd'ya expect? But I've calmed down now, and I've had time to think. And I reckon, if Candy wants to be with you rather than me, that's up to her, isn't it?'

'I'm glad you're beginning to see reason, Daniel,' I say. 'Candy and I are in love. I'm sorry if that hurts you, but there's nothing any of us can do about it –'

I'm cut off as Blister swerves round a corner hard enough to throw me into the door.

'So don't be calling things off with Candy cause you're scared I'm gonna have ya for nicking my bird, right? Far as I'm concerned, we're straight, right?'

'Right,' I say, waiting for the punchline. Or just the punch.

It doesn't come. He just says, 'Your stop, I believe?'

I get out of the car. I can't believe it. As I walk up to the door of the pub, I'm thinking: Daniel Blister making peace and giving me a lift to the gig. Daniel Blister saving my neck. I can't believe it.

I go up to the entrance, and stand to one side for a bunch of kids to come out. I'm thinking: but then again, such are the miracles that come to your aid, if the Dear Lord God and all His glory is with you.

And as I watch the bouncer reach out to grab a bottle of beer from one of the kids, I'm thinking: and the Dear Lord God is always on your side, so long as your accounts are clear.

And I watch the kid slip away from the bouncer, and drain his bottle, and then throw it away. I watch the bottle as it sails through the air and spirals down towards the ground, where it will surely smash into a thousand pieces and do someone an injury before the night is through. I watch, thinking: and of course, I've taken care of everything, I've fixed every last thing –

I watch, as the bottle comes spinning down, and lands safely in a rubbish bin, and the kid winks at the bouncer and walks off. He just walks off. Like he hasn't got a care in the world. Like his accounts are totally clear.

I duck into an alleyway.

He falls to his knees, clasps his hands, eyes shut.

Dear Lord God, I'm really, really, really sorry about dropping the Coke bottle and littering Your beautiful creation, but if You can just fix it for me to win tonight then I promise I'll go straight round there and put it in the bin. Plus, also, I think You'll find that littering is strictly only an offence against the laws of the land, and not as such a sin against You. And I've never ever done it before. Apart from that bubble gum when I was six. Lots of love, Mathew D. Melody, Amen.

And I stay there, listening, just hoping to hear the song of God telling me it's going to be OK but –

– I don't hear anything.

I *feel.*

I feel this pressure on my shoulder –

– and when I open my eyes –

– there's this bloke standing over me.

'Pete?' he says.

He responds to the name as if it is his own.

'What d' you want?' I say.

'Look,' he says, 'I've just gotta tell you . . . look, mate, I'm leaving town tonight, all right and –'

'I don't know who you are,' I tell him, 'but I think you should realise I am not a person who will put up with name-calling. So you can just stop calling me Pete right now. I'm not Pete. I'm Mathew D. Melody.'

'Look, will you just come for a drink with me?'

'I will not,' I tell him. 'I'm sorry if you're feeling lonely, but I'm afraid I have things to do.'

'But there's things I've got to say –'

'And you're going to have to say them to someone else, because I've got a karaoke competition to be winning, and I'm already late for my slot and –'

And this bloke grits his teeth. He takes the Dear Lord's name in vain, several times. He says, 'Look, I'm going, all right: can't you just forget about that karaoke bull . . . for five minutes?'

He draws himself up to his full height.

I stand up.

Beat.

I look him in the eye. He flinches. He looks away. He can't meet my gaze. I say to him, 'Karaoke may be *bullshit* to some people, but it matters to me, and I am not going to give it up for the likes of you!'

I dive into the pub, and I realise – that's it. That's the sign from God. People who *I don't even know*, coming up and wanting to talk to me – that's what happens when you're famous. It's a premonition. It's a prophecy.

I push through the crowd, and there, stage-front, Candy is waiting for me, beautifully turned out in her best moleskin miniskirt and black leather basque.

'Where the – heck – have you been?' she squeals. 'He was gonna give your place to someone else!'

The compère is announcing me.

'Precious,' I say, 'you know I don't approve of such language.'

'I'm sorry, darlin,' she says. 'I was just worried about you. This is your day, and I was just worried about you.'

'I know you were, darling, and it means a lot to me.'

'So . . . did you get to the doctor's?'

'Well, that's what I wanted to tell you,' I say. 'You're going to be very proud of me. The doctor said I was doing much better, and I told him you'd been weaning me off the pills, keeping them safe for emergencies. And so he said I could come off them if I wanted to: and I told him I wanted to.'

She stares at me.

'You what?'

'I told him I can get by without those crutches. I've got my girl and my music. And that's all I need. You've given me the strength to do without the pills.'

She's overcome with joy. 'You've done *what?*'

'I couldn't have done it without you, darling,' I tell her – and then the tape rolls, and it's my tune they're playing. I grab the mike from the compère's hand and jump on stage.

Croons at breakneck speed:

'YanevercloseyureyesanymorewhenIkissyuhlips . . . '

I settle into the rhythm.

Clicks his fingers lounge-lizard style, trying to find the beat.

'and there's no tenderness like before in your fingertips . . .'

And I look into Candy's loving eyes.

Pulls up sharply.

Except . . . they don't – look that loving. They're almost cold. Almost . . . contemptuous.

She's standing there, just in front of the stage, staring at me with these terrible cold eyes, slowly shaking her head . . .

I keep on singing but it has to be the worst performance of my life, cause I'm not feeling the music, I'm not even thinking about the music, I'm just thinking, Candy, Candy, what have I done wrong? How can you look at me with . . . *hatred* in your eyes? How? How?

My heart breaks.

I feel it breaking, like the ice on a lake when some little fat kid tries to go skating. And as that cold stare burns into me, I feel my heart freezing over, like the little fat kid turning blue at the bottom of the lake, and I know I will never love again.

The song comes to an end. Candy turns and walks out of the pub.

I hang my head. My life . . . is over.

And the crowd erupts into applause. The compère puts his arm around me, and there are tears in his eyes, and the thick lenses of his glasses magnify the tears so they're the size of marbles, and in the marbles I can see little rays from the spotlights, splitting up into all the colours of the rainbow, like the rainbow the Dear Lord God sent to Noah after the Flood, to tell him that the bad times were over and everything would be good from now on.

'Mathew,' says the compère. 'You were tremendous in the first heat, yeah, but that was spectacular. I don't think I've heard such an emotional reading of that song – in my life.'

And I begin to understand.

The compère's still going on.

'I don't think we need to,' he says. 'No. I don't think I can *bear* to hear any more. Nothing I could hear tonight could match that performance. That's it. That's it, everyone – the competition is over. Mathew D. Melody – you are the first ever Boar's Head Karaoke King!'

He sees the light.

She pretended! Candy pretended! She *pretended* she didn't love me any more – and scared me into giving the performance of my life.

She put herself through that . . . *torture*. For me.

'Thank you,' I say to the compère. 'Thank you very much indeed. But now, if you'll excuse me, I've got to go. First, I've got to go and put a dangerous bottle safely away in a bin. And then I've got to go and find my true love.

'I've got to go and find my true love – and make her my wife.'

3: don't die just yet

Russell Markham *picks himself up off the floor, nursing a hangover to die from. He pulls out a pack of cigarettes and lights up, holding the filter between thumb and forefinger.*

I think I'd like to end up in America. I admire Americans, cause they'll be on the phone and when the talk gets too much it's just, I gotta go, and that's it. They get bored with a conversation or a situation or a relationship, and it's just, I have someplace I have to be. Someone pisses them off, and they just say,

'Oooh. Fuck you. Your mamma too. *And* your daddy.'

They actually say that. I've heard them with my own ears, so I know it to be the case.

I'm crap at all that. Anything even faintly confrontational, and I'm . . .

He veers away from the end of the sentence.

. . . Woah. No way. I end up just getting very heavily into avoidance behaviour and making excuses; and then I end up letting people bully me into doing stuff I don't really want to. I say, I've got to go, and they say – stay and have another drink.

I say – but I've got to get up in the morning.

And they say – what the fuck for?

And I say – there's this song I've been working on. I was gonna finish it off in the morning.

And they just nod at me.

I end up going the full fifteen rounds. I end up wrecked to the point of brain-death, barely in control of my limbs and pissed off with me, them, her, everybody, every fucking body in this piece-of-shit little town. But saying . . . nothing.

Most of the time, that pissed-offness just sublimates and sinks deep inside; manifesting externally as insomnia, chilblains, vulnerability to coughs, colds and the top ten viruses raging in the wild that week, plus – in the very worst cases – impotence and-forward-slash-or premature ejaculation.

But sometimes, it doesn't sublimate. Sometimes, it festers. It festers, and thickens, and brews itself up into a flammable mix and – explodes. In a rather unpleasant passive-aggressive mess.

So, for example, last night.

We were arguing. We must've been arguing, cause – what else do we do?

I said to her, 'Darlin, I've decided. I'm going. I'm leaving next week.'

And she thought for a moment, and said, 'Well, that's a pity. Billy at work was telling me about this holiday in Cyprus he saw on the teletext. Three hundred quid for a fortnight with as much as you can drink and your own en suite to throw up in.'

'Well,' I said, 'well, that is a pity.'

'Yes,' she said, 'it certainly is.'

Beat.

I was a little surprised at how well she'd taken it, but I didn't want to push my luck. So I scarpered.

I jumped into the shower, and when I came out . . .

. . . She was there. On the phone in front of the telly. At the tail-end of a call, handing over my credit-card details.

'Darling,' I says to her, 'what's going on?'

'Well, it's a limited offer, isn't it. You act, or you miss out.'

'But,' I say to her, 'I thought I said –'

She gets up. 'You said that it was impossible for you to move away next week, and come on holiday with me –'

She walks over towards me.

'– So naturally I interpreted that as meaning you were going to put off your departure, in order that we could go on holiday together.'

She cradles my face in her hands.

'Are you telling me, darling, that my natural interpretation of you was incorrect? Are you saying, darling, that I just . . . don't understand you?'

He crumbles, averts his eyes.

'No, I'm just saying – it's a pity, isn't it, that offers like that don't come up more often.'

'It certainly is a pity.'

She lets go of my face.

'You're looking a bit shaky, darling,' she says. 'Are you all right?'

'Fine,' I say. 'Just a bit . . . just a bit of a glucose crash coming on, I think.'

'Well,' she says, 'you go and get dressed, and I'll serve up. Bit of dinner'll sort your sugar levels out for you.'

I go into the bedroom where my – *posh clothes* – are laid out for me. I put them on and try to scrape some nerve together.

In the kitchen, she's laying the table for dinner. I say, 'Darling, it's just, if I say I'm going to leave, then I kind of have to, don't I? I've sort of made a promise to myself, haven't I? It's like – a debt of honour.'

She doesn't even look up. 'Well, I don't see that at all, darling,' she says. 'There's no reason –' and she slams down my plate

'– why you should –' and she slams down her plate

'– go next week –' and she slams down my fork

'– rather than –' and she slams down her fork

'– in two weeks' –' and she slams down the salt cellar

'– TIME –' And she slams down the red sauce, the brown sauce, the butter dish and the toothpicks.

He steels himself.

'Well, darling –'

And then she does it. She looks up at me.

He crumbles again.

'Well, darling,' I say, 'I suppose you're right, aren't you. I mean, I suppose the whole idea of making a promise to yourself, it's just ridiculous. You know, a promise, it's like inherently something you make to someone else –'

She cuts him off.

'I just want us to have some proper time together before you go away. Sun, sand, sea and . . . other things that begin with "s". And you can bring your guitar and get a bit of practice in. Serenade me on the beach as the sun goes down . . . It'll be dead romantic.'

She hovers over me, thinking. She hovers, not dressed to go out yet, still in vest and combats and bare feet, thinking she's having private, clever thoughts, but even without looking at her face, just from the angle of her hand against her hip I can tell what she's thinking. She's thinking about jumping me. She's still thinking about it as she heads back into the kitchen, favouring me with a sly backward glance just as the strap falls down her shoulder, as she brushes a stray lock of fringe from out her eyes, I can see it –

– even as she brings out the spuds I can see right into her brain, to the very bioelectric flows which *are* her thinking that, armpit stubble notwithstanding, she's looking pretty damn sexy in an unaffected, tousled sort of a way and maybe right now's the moment to take me by surprise and because maybe if it's by surprise then there won't be a chance for me to work up any performance-related anxiety and so maybe this time it'll all happen –

– and I want to shout at her, 'No! No! It won't happen, cause it won't be by surprise, because how can it be by surprise when I can already see you thinking about it, you dull bitch.'

But obviously I can't shout anything like that, so to head her off what I do is, I grab the paper, and as I do so I knock a neat stack of junkmail from the sideboard – and onto the floor. And of course I bend down straight away to retrieve the assorted handbills and flyers –

– but I leave one there.

A cheaply printed pamphlet, a religious tract. I leave that one right there on the floor.

She sees what I've done. Just left it there. On her clean floor.

And that tells her.

I sit back and dive into the paper, hoping for refuge from the dark looks that will be waiting for me if I dare venture a glance her way.

I milk some amusement from the desperate and lonely ads: 'Not Too Dull for Love – cuddly guy, age 48, gets on with parents, children and animals, interests daytime TV and those ornamental plates you get on approval from Sunday supplements, looking for – anyone really. Single mothers and any race accepted.'

But then my eye, expressly without permission, flicks onto a story.

I read the story, and the ground shifts under me.

There's this bloke, lives on the council estate the other side of town. He is what they call a pigeon fancier. He's long been renowned within pigeon-fancying circles for the extraordinary homing skills of his pigeons: and now – in death – they're lending him a small measure of general-purpose local celebrity.

See, the bloke let his pigeons out for a little bit of a flutter, and only one of them came home. It came home in the post. In two separate Jiffy bags. Head in one, body in the other.

The bloke assumed some evil-doer who's savvy to the pigeon-fancying world had kidnapped his birds, and that a ransom note with threats and demands would follow; and that if he paid up – and never fear, he would've paid up – he'd get his pigeons back

Sure enough, the next day, the note came.

Except it wasn't a ransom note. It was more an . . . explanatory note.

And, sure enough, he got his pigeons back. In a number of blood-soaked Jiffy bags. All their necks neatly snapped.

The note said – I mean, it doesn't matter what the note said, because all it could do was confirm the obvious – that the guy responsible was a fucking loon – but the gist was that the loon had seen the pigeons, and tried to feed them some Jelly Babies, and they hadn't been interested in the Jelly Babies.

The loon took this as a sign of an excessively judgemental attitude on their part.

And he decided to illustrate to them the thrust of the Bible's exhortation to us all not to judge, lest we be judged ourselves. The loon did this by *judging* the strength of the pigeons' neckbones against the strength of his hands. And their neckbones were found wanting.

The loon hoped the pigeon fancier would be comforted by the thought that his pigeons had now been learned, and would surely enjoy pigeon heaven.

So there we go. I turn to the local rag hoping for a few cheap laughs at the expense of 'Mr Average Looking For Love'. And I get . . . this.

I look up from the paper, and into her eyes. She's leaning over the now comprehensively laid dinner table, regarding me affectionately.

'Tuck in,' she says. 'You don't want to let it go cold, do you?'

'I'm not eating it,' I tell her.

'And why not?' she says.

And I want to say: because I can't stay a second longer in a town where this kind of stuff goes on.

I want to say to her: it's not about going off and making it as a lovelorn sad-eyed star sailor with a guitar in my hand and a million songs in my broken heart because, as we all know, I'm never going to be any good at playing the guitar. My fingers are too short and stubby, and I can't get them all on one fret at the same time, and I can't even sing and when I try to sing and play together it's like a ZX Spectrum trying to run Windows 2000, it's just too much to cope with all at once.

I want to say to her: it's not about me going away to do something. It's just about me needing to get out of this fucking place.

'Why?' she says. 'Why don't you want to eat the dinner I have lovingly prepared for you?'

'Because,' I tell her, 'because –'

'– Because you've gone and done the mash all creamy again, haven't you? You know I hate it when you do the mash all creamy!'

'Well,' she says, 'you don't have to eat it then, do you, darlin. So long as you eat the rest of your veg.'

I sit there, and play with my unpleasantly creamy mashed potatoes, till I catch her staring at me. I take the hint. I lift a fork laden with mash to my mouth, I ram it home, and I swallow it all down.

'That wasn't so bad, was it?' she says, and smiles.

'No,' I say, and I smile back, 'and by the way, after dinner I've got to leave town.'

Beat.

'Well, I know that,' she says.

No explosion. No shouts of anguish. No incoming cutlery missiles.

I look up at her.

'Well, *of course* I know that,' she says. 'And do you know how come I know? It's because you've told me you've got to leave town about three or four –'

And for a moment it's like her mind disconnects and all the life goes out of her face, and I'm staring at her thinking, I understand now. You're an alien. You've been sent here to test the human male under stress conditions and are tormenting me not out of sadism but in the name of alien science – and when your mind drifts off like that in the middle of an argument, it's because you've gone drifting through a wormhole in the curled-up ninth dimension of spacetime to reach out to the motherworld and dump a particularly juicy new set of experimental data –

And then she slips back into normal space and picks up right where she left off.

'– I know that because, well, I won't say you've said it three or four hundred times a day, because that would be exaggerating, but three or four dozen times a day, definitely. You've said it to me three or four dozen times a day, every day we've been going together.'

'So what do you *think* about me leaving?' I ask her.

'I think,' she says, and she just pats her mouth with her napkin –

Back to her voice, sarcastic.

'No, it's not a napkin, darlin, it's a serviette, because a napkin is a piece of cloth but this is paper, so this is a serviette, darlin –'

Back to his own voice, getting worked up.

– She just dabs at her lips with her serviette, and – why? Why would you do that? It's not like if there was any food stuck to your lips this genteel little dabbing would do a damn thing about it, you need a proper wipe, don't you, to get stuff off your lips, you need a good wipe to get your mouth clean.

Recovering himself.

So she dabs at her lips, and gets up, and says:

'What do I think? I think I would like some peaches and cream for my sweet, that's what I think. Would you like some also, darlin?'

'No, no, I do not want peaches and cream. I don't like peaches and fucking cream.'

'Well, your mum always gives it you every time we're round hers.'

'Well, my mum is a doddering old cow who never listens, isn't she. I don't like peaches, for one, and I don't like cream, for another. I don't even like the artificial cream out of cans that scientists have worked on for decades to make it better than real cream. I don't like any kind of cream product.'

She stands, looking down on me.

'What's so wrong with this place, huh?' she says. 'I mean, you've got a good job.'

And I want to say to her –

Good job? Is that what you think? You think it's a good job, being a supermarket trainee manager, trainee under a glue-sniffing sixteen-year-old who gets write-ups in the local rag for his programme to employ mentally defective young ladies and thus reintegrate them usefully into the community . . . What the write-up does not mention is the real bonus of employing these confused young ladies is how handy they are for a crafty grope off in the warehouse – you can do whatever you like and even if they do cry, you slip them a Mars bar afterwards and that six-year-old's smile is back tattooed on their lips and in their eyes. Cause, after all: you've got to have some perks what with the pay being so shite and work so unspeakably fucking tedious . . .

But I don't say any of that. I just say, 'I'm leaving.'

'And it's not as if we're starving or freezing to death,' she says.

And I want to say – It's not that I'm starving, it's that I eat nuked 99p lasagne six nights a week and whatever's on special for Sunday. And I know I'm not freezing, it's just I can't concentrate on anything but the tick-tick-tick of the meter wheel speeding up whenever I do put the fire on.

But I don't say any of that. I just say, 'I'm leaving *tonight*.'

'And we've got our health, haven't we,' she says.

And I want to say – I know I'm not dying of some banal dehydration disease that could be bought off with a 10p mix of sugars and salt – but I also know that every day I live this shitty life is part-payment on some ultra-complicated physical or mental fuckup thirty years down the road. And I know that when my name finally reaches the top of the fuckup waiting list, I'll actually be grateful. I'll reach down and fondle the tumour-roots growing out of my belly, and say: thanks, guys. Thanks for getting me out of this one.

But I don't say any of that. I just say, 'I'm leaving, tonight, right now.'

And she says, 'And we've got *us*, haven't we? And we love each other, don't we?'

And I want to say – If you knew. If you had half an idea what that word meant. If you even *liked* me or at least didn't hate me and just vaguely wished me well then you'd *help me* for fuck's sake –

He cuts himself off.

But I don't say any of that. I don't get a chance to. Because –

– It's like as I'm thinking it she sees the thought form in my brain and she says, 'I can't believe you're going to let Mickey down. He's been planning this party for ages. And just cause of some stupid story in the paper.'

I get up.

'*Corrie*'s on, darlin,' she says. 'We always cuddle up and watch *Corrie* together.'

I don't say a thing.

'And I've just put the tumble dryer on,' she says. 'It'll be done in an hour – don't you wanna take your clean clothes with you?'

I go into the bedroom and realise if I'm going to pack I need a suitcase.

'You're just stressed out,' she says. 'I'll give you a nice back rub, calm you down.'

I find my suitcase under the stairs. I pull it out and drag it into the lounge. She follows me. She goes to follow me into the bedroom, but – she can't manage it. As she passes the sideboard she has to stop, even at a time like this she has to stop, and lean down and reach for that grubby little flyer I left on the floor to piss her off, and she has to pick it up and neatly fold it into halves and quarters and eighths before putting it away into a drawer.

'Listen,' she says. 'If you're gonna go cause of some stupid story in the paper, then before you go, I wanna tell you a story, and you've gotta listen. And if you listen, I'll let you go.'

'OK,' I say.

'OK,' she says. 'This story used to go around school when I was a kid, one of those stories you hear again and again, only with different names every time. The version I heard when I was in the second year was that Bungle caught a couple of first years going through his jazz-mag stash behind the metalwork block. Bungle reminded the kids that behind the metalwork block was strictly out of bounds to all pupils apart from him and his mates – and so these kids were for it.

'But Bungle offered the kids a deal. They could have the shit kicked out them really really badly . . . or they could provide a little entertainment for Bungle and his mates.

'Noting their interest in German porn, Bungle got them to pick out which picture they liked best, and said they had to jerk off over it with Bungle and all his mates watching and placing bets, or get the shit kicked, really really badly. Now the first kid thinks – fuck it. He wants to swing for Bungle there and then and, fine, get the shit kicked out of him but at least come out of it with his honour intact. So the first kid looks to his friend, ready to kick off and go down in a blaze of glory – and sees in his friend's eyes only horror and terror.

'The first kid looks at his friend and realises his friend would do anything rather than stand up to Bungle.

'So the first kid agrees. For the sake of his friend.

'The friend came in five seconds flat. Obviously appreciated an audience, Bungle said. But the first kid was having problems. So Bungle made his friend help him out. Orally, as it were. And when the first kid finally comes, Bungle says it's not fair one of the kids gets a mouthful and not the other. So he says the first kid, the kid who wanted to fight, has got to lick his friend's jism up off the picture in the porn mag – that, or they'll both get their faces stamped on.

'And the kid does it. Not cause he's scared of getting kicked in by Bungle, but cause his friend is.

'The two kids promise they'll never ever tell anyone about what happened and never ever talk about it again.

'But when they go back for afternoon registration, there's fucking chaos. Someone's stuck a page from a porn mag on the form-room door. And as the caretaker scrapes it off, he's going on all the time about what a strange glue the nasty little vandals have used. A strange glue with an unmistakable, and yet somehow unplaceable smell . . .

'The kid who wanted to fight runs away that afternoon. They catch him, of course, but he can't take the teasing and name-calling. He starts getting into scraps and screaming at his teachers, and in the end his mum gives up and social services take him. But the other kid sticks it. He sticks it out and he never says a word. When the other kids laugh at him, he pretends he can't hear them. When the whole class teases him, he ducks his head in his book so they won't see he's crying. He sticks it out till the school finds something else to gossip about – which takes quite a while, as you can imagine.

'And,' she says, 'it strikes me, if a person didn't have the nerve to leave town after that kind of humiliation, well: that kind of person's never going to leave, are they? They might talk about it, and dream about it, and make plans about it . . . but they'll never actually find the nerve to just get up and go.'

He stands, itches, licks at his lips, wipes his mouth.

'So,' she says to me, 'shall we go down the pub for a drink before we head on to Mickey's party?'

Beat.

In the pub we are instantly crushed. She vanishes and is back in less time than it takes to even walk to the bar with a round of drinks. She puts the first pint in my hand and leans close, and whispers, 'I put a double in it to keep you happy.'

I take a massive gulp and it doesn't do enough so I'm begging her: please stay with me, stay with me just this once – but she's off. 'Just a couple of friends I wanna talk to, darlin.' And she winks at me, and strides off, the crowd parting before her.

I'm like a twat, stapling my elbows to my sides, trying not to take up space, trying to present a low profile and avoid eyes but Mickey swoops in, wondering when he's gonna be able to sort me and the old lady out with a gorgeous little starter home on the new development and how it's shameful a man of my age isn't already several steps up the property ladder – and with the sweaty, hairless chickenflesh pressing against me I know this drink won't be enough, but I haven't got the nerve to deal with the bar and I'm trying to get her attention, trying to get her to talk to me, but she's busy flirting clique to clique, and so I think to myself, maybe, maybe if I put this pint down in one, then in the ten to fifteen seconds immediately after – while my body is still not quite up to speed, still not quite dealing with what I'm doing to it – I might make it to the bar, I might push my way through, I might get served with enough to keep me going till public opinion decides that it's time to go on to Mickey's party.

So I down the pint and stagger straight for the bar –

– and straight into this guy who spins round to face me, and he goes

He covers his face.

He goes –

'Oh my God! It's you!'

And it was . . . this guy from school. I think I recognised this guy . . . Nicholas, from school.

'Listen,' he says to me, 'you were always brainy, I need to ask you something.'

And then she comes over. It's like she's been watching even though I haven't seen her looking my way once. She's spotted I've got someone to talk to and I'm not completely miserable and she's buggered if she's having that.

'We're ready to go,' she announces.

'Well, I'm just talking to my mate,' I tell her, 'and we just wanna have a little chat.'

'Well, I'm ready to go,' she says. She states.

I just look at her.

'I can't leave now, darling,' I tell her. 'My friend here wants to ask me something, and so it would be the height of rudeness to leave just now, wouldn't it?'

'Fine,' she says, 'I'll see you at Mickey's.'

And she flounces off.

She leaves me to walk from the pub to the party on my own. She leaves me to walk from here to Mickey's house which is up Wyndham Street, along Adare Street, up Caroline Street, and along Nolton Street, and Nolton Street's a bugger especially. Especially in the dark. The street lights are half not working, I know this for a fact, and so anybody can come at you from any angle.

I turn back to Nicholas. 'So,' I say to him, trying to keep a lid on it. 'So . . . what was it you wanted to ask me?'

The guy says, 'I want to tell you a story, and when I've finished, I'm going to ask you a question: is the story beautiful, or is it sad?

'The story runs as follows: I'm back in town for a friend's funeral. This friend of mine went to university and worked diligently and got a job straight after, pausing only for a brief summer break in France before getting down to his working life. He got this job that took him away from our town and all the obvious cities, out to a country in the Pacific Rim where he worked for a company that had a licence to print money. That is to say, they printed cash for states too poor to afford the high technology involved in printing secure, forgery-proof currency. Everyone was surprised. We all thought this guy would go places – but spiritual places, saintly places. We all thought he'd do things for humanity, not for cash. But he just got rich, and yet somehow stayed hollow, as if material success meant nothing to him. Which really pissed me off, I have to admit – it was like he was simultaneously exceeding and demeaning all my small-town dreams of ridiculous, vulgar wealth. So it was a grand day for me when finally cash was abolished, and replaced with mood-sensitive, money cards. No fucked-up third-world nations needed to print their own currency any more, and my friend's company became obsolete overnight.

'My friend took early retirement and within a year he was diagnosed as having terminal cancer.

'I went to the hospital to see him, and I said to the doctor, how come, doc? He was always so ferociously healthy. And the doc said, "Kid, it's a psychic thing. He's been carrying this cancer for thirty years, but he always had this passion for his work, and that kept fighting the cancer off. And then he lost what made his life worth living, and his body just gave up."

'So, nervously, I admit, because physical decay really does disgust me, I went in to see my friend, and I said, what the hell's up with you? If your job was keeping you alive, why the hell don't you just get another job?

'And then my friend told me the real and truthful story of his life.

'That summer in France between university and the Pacific Rim he met a girl, a perfect girl with blue eyes and copper hair, and they had an affair. It lasted just long enough for them to fall in love, but not long enough to argue or have a disappointing sexual experience. But this girl was engaged to some cheery, self-starting graduate hardbody and my friend was already booked on a flight to the Pacific Rim. My friend was willing to cancel the flight, but apparently this chick was not willing to cancel the engagement.

'And this totally fucked the guy up. He tasted perfection and had it taken away from him. He tasted how real and connected it was possible to feel and then had it stolen away.

'So he gave up. Twenty-one, the springtime of his life, and he decides he's through with love. He devotes himself to the empty and soon-to-be-obsolete cash trade purely out of this huge existential sulk with the world.

'And what I need to know is: this obsession, your whole existence revolving around somebody you can never actually touch – is that beautiful, or is it tragic?'

Back to **Russell***'s voice.*

You risk life and limb when you confront total fucking nutters like that with too much reality. It can get very messy. What you need is months and months of painstaking counselling to gradually guide them back down to our world. So I don't even attempt an answer. I just make my apologies and back slowly away – but he grabs me and says, 'Look, you've gotta fucking answer me, OK, because of course, there is no friend, there is no guy, everything I've been telling you about, it's me, it's my life – I've wasted the last thirty years and now I've got cancer for a skeleton and only the fact that my blood is saturated with pharmaceutical coke is keeping me from going mad with the pain. And what I need to know is, this girl, this perfect girl who, if you must know, had copper hair like a newly minted penny and eyes as blue as a fiver – if I call her up and tell her my whole empty life has been a tribute to her, no, not even a tribute, it's just been a shell, a mould, a casing around the vacuum where our love should have grown –

'– will she laugh at me, or will she think it's beautiful?'

I pull the guy's hands off me, and I say, 'What the fuck? What do you mean, you've wasted the last thirty years? You're the same age as me. We were at school together.'

'Yeah,' he says. 'We were at school together.'

'But you're fucking fifty,' I say to him. 'You're fifty years old and you're dying of cancer.'

'Yeah,' he says.

'And that can't be,' I tell him, ''cause you're the same age as I am. And I'm twenty-three.'

And he starts slowly to back away from me, his eyes full of something unspeakable and bad, that look you get when you realise the friendly stranger you've been chatting to all night is actually an escaped psychotic and your life may now be in danger because you've accidentally confronted him with a little more reality than he can handle. He backs away from me, hands up, saying, 'No, no, you were twenty-three, you were twenty-three, but hell, so was I once . . .'

I grab him and say, 'No, you fucking lunatic, I'm no way fucking fifty, for Christ's sake. Do you think I wouldn't've noticed wasting fifty years pissing around this shithole of a town? Do you think I wouldn't have noticed the fucking decades passing?'

He slowly collapses, easing himself down to the floor, lying down, curling up, making himself small.

I open my eyes I don't know how much later. But when finally I do open my eyes, I am back at my place, I'm on the floor, I can't feel my legs my arms nothing, just this pain in my guts like . . .

Beat.

There was this story that went round our school, about these two kids, these two best mates who got caught looking at Bungle's jazz-mag stash behind the metalwork block.

Bungle really just . . . did bad things to them. One of the kids had wanted to fight Bungle: the other . . . didn't have the nerve. The kid who'd wanted to fight couldn't stand the shame, and – so the story goes – ran away and no one knows what happened to him.

The story's wrong, of course. His mum knows what happened to him. The doctor that prescribed the sedatives knows what happened to him. The nurses that shaved his head . . . they know. His best mate . . . he knows. But what can he do? He didn't have the nerve to fight and save his friend, he doesn't have the nerve to run and save himself. So he's fucked too.

So there we go. A sad little epilogue to a sad story, which just makes it . . . sadder still.

Unless, of course, it doesn't end there. Who knows? I mean, maybe, maybe the kid who didn't have the nerve to run, didn't have the nerve to fight, maybe he had the nerve to wait.

And maybe – say, maybe the kid woke up one day and found out Bungle had been picked for the Under-18s team, picked to play against England. And maybe he called on a schoolboy classic; maybe he dosed Bungle's sandwiches with an immense amount of over-the-counter laxative.

And if that did happen, then when Bungle ran out onto the hallowed turf to represent his school and his nation, and the entire contents of his intestines moved abruptly and explosively into his shorts – that wasn't just a random tragedy, it was a carefully planned act of revenge.

Surely: when the arrogance on Bungle's face dissolved into bewilderment, into horror, into . . . sobbing and tears and moans of anguish, and with one hand pressed pathetically against his arsehole as if to stem the flow, Bungle ran from the field, back down the tunnel, a foul-smelling yellow liquid spilling from his shorts as he ran; and when the school, and the nation lost, and Bungle lost his nerve, and he never played again and left school shortly after, and a promising sporting career was ruined – surely, that would be enough to settle the score.

And if the score was settled: then one day, wouldn't the kid finally wake up and realise the story had come to an end, and he could finally move on.

He sits up.

I come to, and I'm back at the flat; and in front of me is my suitcase. It is packed. I, apparently, have packed it. It seems I'm ready to go.

I phone for a taxi and they promise to get me to the station in time for my train or give me double my train fare in compensation.

I can go. Escape is allowed. It's not only allowed; there are systems in place to ensure my escape goes smoothly.

I get to the station in good time. All I have to do is wait for the train: and get on it. I'm free to leave.

Except, of course, I can't go without saying goodbye, can I?

Because you can't just leave things like that unsaid, can you? You can't start something new when there's old business still to be sorted.

I – find a guard, and he says he'll watch my suitcase for me.

He crumbles, almost doubles up – like something potentially explosive is happening in his guts but he's in polite company and can't let it show.

I walk into the party and Mickey says, 'Uh, hi. I, uh, your old lady's been working the crowd.'

And I say to him, 'Mickey, who the fuck talks like that? What's wrong with you?'

And he says, 'Look, it's just . . . I think – I think she's, you know, caught some action in your absence.'

And I follow his eyes, and I see her –

– talking to this fucking –

– this beery cunt with a chunky gold choker –

– actually talking to this cunt with mangled teeth, and a drooling mouth, and a heavy, unbroken eyebrow crowning his perpetually broken nose, casting deep, deep shadows over the layered bags around his eyes –

– royal-blue bags folding into purple bags, which fold into dark-brown bags, which melt into his glassy, bottomless, granite eyes –

– and her assuming the classic pose – leaning slightly into the curve of his body, secondary sexual organs –

Breast-cupping gesture.

– presented, hand resting lightly on his forearm, whispering to him, lowering her voice so he has every excuse to lean in closer, so with every word her sweet breath caresses his left-over cauliflower ear –

Clutching at his belly.

– and, oh, the smile blossoming over his idiot face as she speaks –

Doubling over, actually moaning, then looking up.

And then she's at my side, saying, 'Honey, are you all right? Honey, what's wrong?'

And I'm just babbling, just – 'I can't believe what you're doing. I can't believe you'd – with that fucker!'

'Well, darlin,' she says, 'if you're gonna leave me, if you're gonna leave town, I'm gonna have to find someone to look after me, aren't I?'

I look up at him and his gaze swings around the room, and
– I turn away.

'All right! All right,' I tell her, 'I'll stay. Just promise me
you're not gonna go anywhere near that bastard.'

'I promise,' she says. 'I promise, if you're gonna stay.'

'I will, just – get me out of here.'

She helps me out onto the street.

'I know you must be shocked, darlin,' she starts, 'but I had
to do something . . . to make you realise how much – just
how hard it'd be for me if you left. I couldn't go on on my
own. I'd have to have someone to look after me.'

We get to the flat. I always open the door, so she waits for
me to pull out my keys. I tell her I haven't got them, I left
them on the table cause I'm leaving now –

– And in her face there's a look of panic which I'm only just
noticing and it strikes me that what she said about needing
someone to look after her wasn't just a line to get me to stay.
I mean, obviously, it was a line, it was a cheap cruel line,
but – not just a line. She really is afraid of being on her own.
Of me leaving.

'Honey,' I say to her, 'I'm not coming in with you.'

'But you promised,' she starts, 'you promised, you little shit,
you lying little piece of shit –'

'I'm not coming in because you're going up to your flat,
you're going to pack a bag, and you're coming with me.'

Her face freezes.

'You're coming with me. We're leaving this shithole tonight,
and tomorrow –'

'You're not leaving me?'

And I smile at her. A real smile, for the first time in ages.

'I can't live here. You can't live without me. So we leave – together.'

And she smiles back.

He straightens up.

She runs up the stairs, in such a rush she forgets to close the door behind her. The light goes on in her flat. I see her silhouette moving against the window as she rushes around the flat, getting her things together. And I'm thinking – maybe this is it. All this time I've been trying to get up the nerve to leave town on my own and perhaps all I needed all along was – to have her with me. All I need is – my girl.

And then the action upstairs stops.

She comes to the window. She leans out.

'Darlin,' she says. 'I can't decide what to take. Will you come up and help me?'

'It doesn't matter,' I say, 'just pack a bag for a couple of days. You can come back and clear your flat out when we're set up, all right?'

She stares down at me.

'Darlin, can't we just stay tonight and go tomorrow?'

'No. If I stay another night in this shithole, I'll never get out. I'm going tonight.'

Her face vanishes from the window.

She comes back. She says, 'Darlin, I'm just filling the bath. I'm gonna get in. And . . . I'm gonna cut myself, and let myself bleed. I'm gonna bleed to death, darlin, unless you come up and save me.'

'I can't, honey,' I tell her. 'I can't come up. I haven't got my key.'

'You don't need it,' she says, 'I made sure the door didn't close behind me. So either you come up, or I'm gonna bleed to death.'

And that's –

– when the bastard hits me. The first thing I know is I'm slammed up against the wall, my nose in bits sliding down my face and my mouth full of snot and blood, and then this cunt is punching hell out my kidneys, screaming, 'What the fuck've you done with her, you fucker? Where the fuck is she?'

I slide down the wall and crash onto the pavement.

'MARY!' he screams, 'MARY!'

'Where the fuck is she? What the fuck have you done with her?'

And he's howling, he's howling like a little baby, 'MARY! MARY!'

And with blood in my eyes I look up and she's there in the window.

He steps towards me, screaming and spitting and –

– a phone goes. His phone goes.

He picks up, and talks, I can see in his eyes that he's going to put the boot in, and it's just scratching an itch to him. I'll see his foot going up, and it'll be in slow motion, obviously, it'll be in slow motion so I'll have time to understand that I'm going to die and he's not going to stop stamping on me till I do die –

– and he puts away his phone and leans down, brings his face very close to mine and whatever he's going to say I don't want to hear it I'd just rather die now please just let me die now rather than have to go through this and he opens his mouth and he says, 'Look, mate,' he says, and I look up and I see things have shifted under the surface of his face.

'Look, mate,' he says –

And I realise I can get out of this alive –

'Look, I'm sorry about that –'

– he wants something from me, and I can give it to him, and I can get out of this alive –

'– just got a bit fucked-up –'

He wants me to look up at him, or shrug, or nod – and let him off the hook –

'Didn't mean anything by it, like –'

And he needs it, he needs this from me –

'And you're all right, aren't you?'

It'll just take one word and I won't have to die.

'No hard feelings, like.' He finds the ghost of a smile. A nervy, edgy, scared, scared smile, as he offers me his hand. I just have to take his hand, and I can have my life back.

Except: I can't.

I can't. Because –

– Because of years of watching my best mate staggering round the place, a chemically coshed wreck of a man who doesn't even remember his own name, let alone mine: because of having to watch the poor bastard singing to himself in pubs and kneeling on streetcorners praying out loud and reading in the paper about him getting done for ripping the necks off fucking pigeons.

His hand hangs in the air, his eyes are pleading: and just by spitting in his face now or even turning away, I can get my fucking head kicked in – but I'll have paid the fucking bastard back.

Beat.

'Cheers, butt,' he says, as his knuckles crush mine. 'Fucking appreciate it.'

'You're all right, mate,' I hear myself saying, 'no fucking worries.'

He walks off, back towards town.

Beat.

I slump down onto the kerb.

At my feet, in the gutter, there's a Coke bottle. An old-fashioned one, a glass one. It glitters with orange in the street lights.

The door to our building swings open. I feel the warmth from the central heating wasting, spilling out onto the street.

Beat.

I find him outside the Boar's, leaning against this crappy Escort van, swearing as he plays some stupid little game on his mobile.

He sees me coming, and puts his phone away.

'For fuck's sake, mate,' he says. 'I thought we were straight, like.'

I keep walking.

'I've apologised about smacking you, and if it's about the girl, then – tough. She wants me and there's fuck all you can do about it.'

'It's not about the girl,' I tell him.

'What?' he says, and he's not even pretending he didn't hear me, he just didn't hear me cause though I thought I was speaking normally, actually, I was whispering, I could barely manage to force the air out and my voice was trembling so bad –

'What did you just say?' he goes.

I take my hand from behind my back, and let him see the bottle.

He looks at me, and he's –

– disappointed. Disappointed in me.

'For fuck's sake,' he says. 'You don't wanna be doing that now, do you.'

I step towards him.

'Look, mate,' he tells me, 'whatever it is, whatever you think it is, you've got the wrong bloke, all right? It wasn't me.'

I smash the bottle on a lamp-post, and raise the jagged shards towards him. His face darkens.

'You didn't wanna do that. You didn't wanna fucking threaten me, you shitehawk.'

I say to him –

I don't say anything, my mouth's so dry I can't say anything, so I just take a step closer.

And he says, 'You didn't wanna fuckin do that, you shitehawk, unless you had the fuckin nerve to go through with it. And you fuckin don't.'

He steps towards me, all apologies gone.

'You don't have the fuckin nerve, boy. You're fuckin gutless.'

He's right, of course, I realise. I don't have the fuckin nerve.

He steps closer and I realise there's no malice in what he's about to do: I've threatened his life, and he just can't permit that. And so, he's going to stamp on my face again and again and again –

He comes a step closer, and I've got three seconds left to live and I'm trying to think of some oh so fucking clever line that's going to humiliate this bastard for ever and follow him for the rest of his life and make up for me and make up for

Pete yet at the same time is not such a clever line that it just shoots uselessly over his empty fucking head –

But as he reaches out to take the bottle from me all I can think of to scream is:

'You've got no fuckin friends, you bastard, everyone pretends to be friends with you cause they're fucking scared of you but everyone takes the piss behind your back, you bastard –'

His face creases, and I just don't have the nerve – and he knows it, he knows me, and I don't have the nerve, and the bottle slips under his chin –

The first point slips into his soft, jowelly throat and I just don't have the nerve –

The glass edge finds a vital artery and blood shoots out all over us, and I'm just a gutless little shitehawk, that's all I am –

And he falls onto his knees and onto the pavement, scrabbling at the flaps in his throat, hissing and gurgling away, and I kneel, and reach out – but I don't have the nerve to do it, I don't have the nerve to actually lay a finger on him –

And so carefully, carefully, so as not to touch his actual skin, I pull the van keys from his hand.

I get into his crappy Escort van. I fire it up and pull a U-turn and drive. And as I'm pushing the pedal as far as it will go I look in the mirror and just catch sight of a figure that might be Mary, gathering him into her arms, screaming and shrieking but then –

– as she pulls his face close to hers, their eyes meet and it seems for a moment like the terror fades from his face and the horror fades from hers and they're both there caught in each other's gaze, and caught in that moment, and in that moment there's no room for horror or terror, only space for something else; so in the space where horror and terror should be there's just a vacuum, and because nature abhors a vacuum some new thing is created to fill the gap between them; and I try to give it a name because there is a word for it, I'm sure; but the word won't come to me now, the word was never there, and as the van pulls away I'm already forgetting them, forgetting that town and that life, and forgetting the hope that a word might ever bridge the gap between us.